Transforming Medical Library Staff for the Twenty-First Century

Medical Library Association Books

The Medical Library Association (MLA) features books that showcase the expertise of health sciences librarians for other librarians and professionals.

MLA Books are excellent resources for librarians in hospitals, medical research practice, and other settings. These volumes will provide health-care professionals and patients with accurate information that can improve outcomes and save lives.

Each book in the series has been overseen editorially since conception by the Medical Library Association Books Panel, composed of MLA members with expertise spanning the breadth of health sciences librarianship.

Medical Library Association Books Panel

Kristen L. Young, AHIP, chair
Dorothy Ogdon, AHIP, chair designate
Michel C. Atlas
Carolann Lee Curry
Kelsey Leonard, AHIP
Karen McElfresh, AHIP
JoLinda L. Thompson, AHIP
Heidi Heilemann, AHIP, board liaison

About the Medical Library Association

Founded in 1898, MLA is a 501(c)(3) nonprofit, educational organization of 3,500 individual and institutional members in the health sciences information field that provides lifelong educational opportunities, supports a knowledge base of health information research, and works with a global network of partners to promote the importance of quality information for improved health to the health-care community and the public.

Books in Series

The *Medical Library Association Guide to Providing Consumer and Patient Health Information* edited by Michele Spatz
Health Sciences Librarianship edited by M. Sandra Wood
Curriculum-Based Library Instruction: From Cultivating Faculty Relationships to Assessment edited by Amy Blevins and Megan Inman
The Small Library Manager's Handbook by Alice Graves
Mobile Technologies for Every Library by Ann Whitney Gleason

Transforming Medical Library Staff for the Twenty-First Century

Edited by

Melanie J. Norton

Nathan Rupp

ROWMAN & LITTLEFIELD
Lanham • Boulder • New York • London

Published by Rowman & Littlefield
A wholly owned subsidiary of The Rowman & Littlefield Publishing Group, Inc.
4501 Forbes Boulevard, Suite 200, Lanham, Maryland 20706
www.rowman.com

Unit A, Whitacre Mews, 26-34 Stannary Street, London SE11 4AB

British Library Cataloguing in Publication Information Available

Library of Congress Cataloging-in-Publication Data

Names: Norton, Melanie J., 1959– editor. | Rupp, Nathan, 1970– editor.
Title: Transforming medical library staff for the twenty-first century /
    edited by Melanie J. Norton, Nathan Rupp.
Description: Lanham : Rowman & Littlefield, [2017] | Series: Medical Library
    Association books series | Includes bibliographical references and index.
Identifiers: LCCN 2017025843 (print) | LCCN 2017048331 (ebook) | ISBN
    9781442272200 (electronic) | ISBN 9781442272194 (hardcover : alk. paper)
Subjects: LCSH: Medical libraries—Personnel management.
Classification: LCC Z675.M4 (ebook) | LCC Z675.M4 T73 2017 (print) | DDC
    025.1/9661—dc23
LC record available at https://lccn.loc.gov/2017025843

♾™ The paper used in this publication meets the minimum requirements of American National Standard for Information Sciences—Permanence of Paper for Printed Library Materials, ANSI/NISO Z39.48-1992.

Printed in the United States of America

To our colleagues at the Yale University Cushing/Whitney Medical Library and the larger health sciences library profession we dedicate this book.

Contents

Foreword

Patricia Flatley Brennan

For the first time in my life, I am the director of a library. Now, it's a special type of library: the National Library of Medicine (NLM), which plays a special role among medical libraries. As the director of the NLM I also serve as part of the leadership of the National Institutes of Health (NIH). The mission of the NIH is to *transform discovery into health*; as the largest biomedical knowledge collection in the world, the NLM provides a platform for discovery. Both the NLM and its parent organization are large, complex institutions that employ thousands of people—so a book such as *Transforming Medical Library Staff for the Twenty-First Century*, which guides leaders to prepare staff for the future, has a ready audience here. And isn't it propitious that I have been asked to provide the foreword to this collection? In particular, because I lead an enterprise that does many of the things that medical libraries do—acquisition, collection management, patron services—this book has very practical, specific guidance for me now.

History tells us that the one persistent characteristic of discovery and health is that both are always changing. Early discoveries of basic biomedical knowledge arose from the experience of clinicians observing the responses of their patients to therapeutics ranging from sunlight to poultices. By the mid-eighteenth century, experimentation supplanted observation as a pathway to discovery, and the evidence base for practice emerged from systemic investigations. By the mid-twentieth century, computation enriched the experimental approaches, allowing faster computation of larger data sets, and accelerated our understandings of the biological, psychosocial, and environmental foundations of health. And now, in 2017, we are entering the data science era. As the substrate of discovery and health changed, so did the nature of what constitutes a library and what are considered essential library services. Each of these changes required that medical library staff develop new skills, change the focus of their work, and balance novel strategies for collections management and dissemination with tried-and-true approaches.

Libraries provide the foundation for discovery and health. Libraries themselves are dynamic organizations, guiding change from within as well as responding to perturbations in the larger environment. Changes in the processes of discovery and health provide a significant impetus demanding that libraries provide new services, reach unanticipated patrons, and serve up new resources for discovery. And each of these changes places new demands on the medical library staff. And this book provides sage guidance to help medical librarians best meet the challenges of the future.

Melanie Norton and Nathan Rupp have gathered great thinkers to impart great wisdom. How do you prepare—even excite—medical library staff for the future? This book provides both a map and an itinerary for medical libraries. The editors and their authors offer an exciting view of the central roles of medical libraries and medical library staff in the future of health and health-care delivery, and then guide the reader through some key steps toward realization of the library of the future. Its themes, both familiar and novel, are presented in an accessible manner—and before you explore the depth of the wisdom presented here, let me provide a few peeks into wisdom:

- Create a culture of empowerment.
- Ensure that jobs have individual meaningfulness and achievable competence.
- Recognize the value of a highly diverse staff (classified, paraprofessional, professional).
- Remember that roles are many times fluid and sometimes lack boundaries.

Yet the authors have avoided a common pitfall of books written to help managers transform staff. Rather than offering descriptions of the idealized staff member of the future—the new jobs, the new skills, the new opportunities—this book takes a different approach, extolling managers to discover and enrich staff members as they embark on the future. Teresa Knott reminds managers that the human resources are the greatest asset of the library, and challenges them to create a culture of empowerment. Later, Dixie Jones warns that roles are fluid and job descriptions lack boundaries. She extolls readers to help staff

Patricia Flatley Brennan

build on their existing skill sets to embrace emerging skills, including flexibility, initiative, and the ability to work with teams and with diverse populations.

And the wisdom does not stop with how to manage staff—there's great guidance for managers themselves: cultivating political skills, investing in engagement, and budgeting skills are important but there may be other skills (like leading in transition) that are even more important. One piece of advice I found particularly important was the need to consider library as a service, not library as a repository. The book nicely builds on the 2003 Association of Research Libraries document "New Roles for New Times: Transforming Liaison Roles in Research Libraries." Although not all medical libraries are research libraries, all academic health science research libraries have a research mission—and because many medical libraries support practice, their service mission is already well-known.

This book is particularly important right now: the reduction of medical libraries throughout our health-care systems requires us to think about how medical librarians can serve when they are not attached to specific libraries, and there is a need to frame the roles of medical librarians separate from presence of medical libraries.

This book targets the managers of medical libraries in a way that guides them toward the future, yet it has wisdom that could be of benefit to the medical librarians themselves, as well to those of us (like me!) whose responsibilities transcend traditional organizations. Explore its wisdom and apply its knowledge—it will help you toward the future.

Preface

Melanie Norton and Nathan Rupp

Entering the main entrance of the Cushing/Whitney Medical Library, one is enveloped in the elegant marble walls and star-spangled ceiling of the front rotunda. Further exploration reveals intricate woodwork, glazed bookshelves, and another rotunda where scientific artifacts are displayed. Amid the historical ambience are rooms with rows of personal computers, indicative of the major transformation this Yale University library has undergone—not unlike other libraries in the digital age.

In the time since we arrived as new hires some five years ago, the changes we have witnessed in the Cushing/Whitney Medical Library and other Yale institutions have been phenomenal. These include the opening of the first residential college in fifty years, physical renovations at the Sterling and Beinecke libraries, and the acquisition by our affiliated teaching hospital's acquisition of another hospital in New Haven—resulting in one of the largest medical facilities in the nation. In our library, the departments we head—access and delivery services, and collection development and management—have also seen significant change. Access and delivery became one department, a major inventory and subsequent transfer of books and journals to off-site storage was completed, and many of our technical services operations were shifted to the main campus library.

As expected, these changes have added to the challenge of managing staff. In addition to the usual modifications to workflow and retirements, we both had staff redeploy to other departments or into a cross-departmental team that typically tackles special projects. Hearing other colleagues in the health sciences community relate their experiences with closures, mergers, staff reductions, and changing patterns of service, we knew this was an area open for examination. We felt that a fresh look at strategies to evaluate, train, motivate, and deploy staff would help medical as well as other library managers become more effective at providing services in the challenging environment of the twenty-first century—a time of unprecedented change. Partnering with our publishers, we compiled and edited ten chapters written by colleagues we thought were particularly well qualified to offer relevant and useful information, and the result is the book before you.

We were fortunate to have Dr. Patricia Brennan contribute a foreword for our book. In her role as director of the National Library of Medicine, she has communicated the need for a new set of skills to operate a successful library in the twenty-first century. In contemplating future goals, close attention to individual employees as well as overall staff development can help ensure success.

In chapter 1, we address the changing environment of medical education and health-care delivery, discuss why medical libraries must remain flexible in adapting to new situations, and provide a broad overview of some of the changes in staffing that need to be considered.

In chapter 2, Teresa Knott addresses the importance of individual and team empowerment, introducing several factors managers should be aware of to foster employees who appreciate self-improvement, feel confident and motivated to make decisions, and realize the positive impact of their work. Discussing relevant terms such as *competence, autonomy, trust, communication,* and *rewards,* she also includes a section on the limits of empowerment.

As technological advances continue to accelerate, the relevance of acquiring knowledge and learning new skills takes on added importance. In an in-depth look at training and professional development, Amy Blevins, Ryan Harris, and Elizabeth Kiscaden open chapter 3 with a summary of the major changes that have occurred in library services. Confirming the need for continuing education while acknowledging the barriers to it, they discuss various avenues to initiate or acquire training and professional development, including examples from a half-dozen university libraries. In-house or outside workshops, online modules, onboarding policies, certification programs, and library associations are some of the ways one can engage in lifelong learning.

Melanie Norton and Nathan Rupp

What is a nimble organization, and what benefits does being nimble confer? In chapter 4, Jean Shipman and Mary Joan (M. J.) Tooey examine this attribute in the realm of libraries, and why it is important, in an era of rapid change, for leaders and staff to identify opportunities, trends, and potential pitfalls and then respond in a decisive manner. Missing positive opportunities or letting problems fester is never a good thing, but creating a nimble work environment can be challenging. The authors describe innovative ways to achieve this, using examples from health sciences libraries, and discuss several factors that impact the ability of an organization to acquire and maintain nimbleness.

What is effective communication? How can managers and staff avoid misinterpreted, forgotten, or poorly designed messages—delivered the wrong way? In chapter 5, Heather Homes, Shannon Jones, and Ana Reeves explore the various styles and methods used to share information in an academic library. With an emphasis on knowing your audience, they discuss various workplace scenarios, the latest technology, and tips to improve communication to create a more successful workplace.

After a strategic planning initiative, the Lamar Soutter Library of the University of Massachusetts Medical School decided their unionized support staff needed restructuring. Given the transformation of the library workplace, their roles had become too narrow, and their ability to crosstrain or learn higher-level skills were restricted. In chapter 6, Elaine Martin explores this midsized library's approach to—and ultimate success in—restructuring its staff. The library involved the staff as a partner from the outset, but first had to persuade them this change was needed and would benefit everyone. Describing insights into what was learned, including the negotiation process, Martin concludes that having a unionized staff needn't be an impediment to restructuring.

How well do you know your staff? In chapter 7, Dixie Jones covers a lot of ground in her research regarding this important question—offering examples from her own experience with staff who went off-script and accomplished novel tasks not strictly in their job descriptions. Especially in today's library environment, it is becoming more critical to have staff who can go beyond their basic job duties. Knowing an employee—his work habits, motivations, strengths and weaknesses, expectations, and hidden talents—can lead to greater flexibility in improving current services or offering new ones, as well as fostering a more satisfying workplace.

Whether it is called *consolidation* or *integration*, a medical library may undergo a merger with its university's main library system. Budgetary and technological pressures may precipitate this reorganization, but is it a good thing? In chapter 8, Gerald Perry and Michael Brewer posit that it can be, using the University of Arizona Libraries (UAL), where they work, as a case study. After careful planning, the merger of the University of Arizona Health Sciences Library with UAL began in 2013. The authors discuss how a newly acquired economy of scale can be leveraged to increase and improve services, while still adhering to budgetary realities. The authors note that staff changes required for mergers—UAL created new managerial roles and used a hybrid liaison model to organize librarians' duties—can be controversial, but if done right, can improve the overall library system with increased efficiencies, flexibilities, and services.

In chapter 9, Meredith Solomon and Meghan Muir reveal the day-to-day reality faced by solo librarians or small staff medical libraries in an era of rapid change. Drawing on their personal experiences working in hospital libraries, they discuss the often unique challenges faced by the librarian toiling alone or with a few staff members. Fast-paced environments, isolation, small budgets, constant interruptions, and loss of space can lead to stress and discouragement. While some of these factors cannot be avoided, the authors offer strategies to mitigate them. They stress the importance of being useful to your clientele, even to the point of seeking out nonusers.

How a manager deals with staff has a direct impact on an organization's success, and the same holds true for medical libraries. How can a manager hire and retain high-performing employees? What steps can be taken to create a more motivated, skilled, diverse, and satisfied workforce? In chapter 10, Shannon Jones explores these questions, discussing staff and self-discovery assessments, recruitment plans, the importance of soft skills and a positive work environment, personal development, mentoring, and the various ways to recognize and reward excellent work.

We have enjoyed working on this book—and with our authors—and hope that it will be a good guide for library managers, especially those in the area of library staffing within medical libraries, as libraries continue to significantly change in the next decade.

Melanie Norton and Nathan Rupp

Acknowledgments

We wish to thank all the chapter authors, our families, and our colleagues at Yale University's Harvey Cushing/John Hay Whitney Medical Library.

Chapter 1

The Changing Environment of Medical Libraries

Melanie J. Norton and Nathan Rupp

In the last twenty years, external factors have changed medical librarianship in significant ways, and these factors will continue to greatly affect librarianship in the coming decades. Cultural, technological, and generational changes have manifested themselves in both educational and health-care settings, so medical libraries have been doubly impacted. Medical libraries need to recognize these factors and their impacts, and organize their staff appropriately. This chapter will use the example of the Cushing/Whitney Medical Library at Yale University to explore several factors that are changing medical libraries and introduce steps library managers may need to take to organize staff in ways that address these changes.

Technological and Generational Changes

The introduction of the Internet nearly one-quarter century ago has increased user expectations, regardless of the type of services or products being delivered. Incoming medical students—our future physicians and medical school faculty—were born during this period and represent the generation that is accustomed to instant results and convenience. Other organizations, such as Amazon, have mastered new levels of efficiency in delivering products and services to customers (package delivery by drone, anyone?).[1] Customers have come to expect similar efficiencies and speed from all organizations with which they interact, including libraries. Changes in user expectations have manifested themselves in a number of ways. Libraries have had to reimagine how they should staff their service desks, considering such questions as whether they should staff their service desks virtually or partner with other libraries around the country to provide virtual services to users outside of normal business hours. Libraries must now emplace staff who ensure that digital content is always up-to-date and accessible. They may have to partner with organizations outside the library that manage special tools, such as the electronic health record system, through which library resources can now be deployed in addition to traditional finding tools like the library catalog. Finally, libraries are now asked to deliver services and provide access to resources wherever users are based, even on the other side of the world.

In addition to changes in user expectations that are driven by technology, many library patrons have asked that libraries provide meditation centers, relaxation centers (including board games), and cafés. These amenities would have been unheard of a generation ago.

Cultural Changes

Another factor in users' increased expectations is their increasingly busy schedules. This is related to the increasing number of single-parent households, households in which both parents work, and the number of children enrolled in extracurricular athletics. For example, the percentage of children living in a home with two married parents in their first marriage declined from 73 percent in 1960 to 46 percent in 2013.[2] Similarly, the percentage of children living in a home with a single parent increased from 9 percent in 1960 to 34 percent in 2013.[3] Meanwhile, the percentage of households where both parents work has increased from 25 percent in 1960 to 60 percent in 2012.[4] Finally, the number of children registered for youth soccer has increased from about 103,000 in 1974 to more than three million in 2014.[5] Due to cultural changes like these, library patrons' schedules are much more compressed than they might have been in the past; as a result, they have less time to interact with library resources and services through studying and research.

Information Delivery

The Internet has dramatically changed the way in which information is delivered, affecting a library's traditional roles. This is seen in several ways. Traditionally, libraries primarily served as repositories of information, storing print monographs and serials for mainly on-site use. In the twenty-first century, their power to disseminate information via the Internet has increased exponentially. Secondly, libraries once provided reference answers via a traditional reference

Melanie J. Norton and Nathan Rupp

collection. Today, would-be library patrons use easy-access websites such as Wikipedia to answer these questions. Libraries are asked to provide support for more in-depth types of research, such as the systematic reviews handled by medical librarians. Libraries also deal with significantly different types of questions regarding information preservation. Where they once dealt with brittle paper and torn bindings for print materials, they now also work with users who are unable to access electronic resources due to vendor system outages, users' misconfigured systems, or library system glitches.

Changes in Medical Education

In addition to these cultural changes, there have been several changes in the institutions with which medical libraries closely work: schools of medicine and allied health, clinics, and hospitals. Some of the most significant changes in medical education include the flipped curriculum, the delivery of medical education to distance learners, increased competition in medical education, and the higher cost of medical school.

Flipped Curriculum

The flipped curriculum entails a change not only in the sequence of classes medical students take, but also in the way they take them. Instead of attending class and listening to a lecture, students are now expected to view lectures online and come to class prepared to discuss them. To this end, medical libraries might hire videographers to help record classes so that students can view them off-line; others have considered whether to hire specialized staff to assist faculty members in using video technology to its fullest potential. Several years ago, one of this book's editors participated in an MBA program that was held via videoconference. Responsibility for the program was shared by faculty at two different universities, one of whom had experience with the technology while the other did not. The instruction from the faculty member who had that experience was markedly better. It is important for institutions engaging in new forms of instruction to get the technology right, and libraries can help in this area. If lectures are being recorded, both for the flipped curriculum and distance education, libraries should maintain high standards for recorded course offerings—for the students' benefit as well as their own reputations.

Distance Education

Another significant change in medical education affecting medical libraries is the delivery of instruction to distance learners. Although distance education is nothing new to academia—with correspondence courses and semesters abroad going back decades—the Internet has revolutionized this type of education, and medical education has not been immune to this revolution. Though the training of physicians is traditionally done on-site, many programs supported by medical libraries—such as the physician associate program offered through Yale's School of Medicine—are now offered online. Delivering library services to distance education learners may require a specific set of skills, such as the ability to provide research deliverables in formats like Microsoft PowerPoint slide decks. It may also require that libraries supporting distance education programs hire librarians to work remotely—closer to the students rather than the home campus. For example, Central Michigan University employs librarians working in Atlanta, Georgia, to assist students enrolled in its Global Campus programs.[6] Libraries delivering services in this way need to take special care to align the services, policies, and programs at the remote locations with those at the home institution, except in cases where the remote locations require services and policies designed specifically for them.

Increased Competition in Medical Education

A third significant change in medical education is increased competition. More MD programs have achieved initial accreditation in this decade than in any decade since the 1970s.[7] Students look at several different factors when choosing a medical school, including residency placement, faculty research interests, and the reputation of the departments representing the discipline in which they are most interested. Another factor they may consider in selecting a medical school is the resources and services offered by its library. As students encounter more schools to choose from, medical libraries will need to stay relevant to students' needs to ensure their schools remain competitive.

Increased Cost in Medical Education

Finally, the cost of medical school tuition has increased significantly over the past quarter century. The average cost of tuition at the top ten research and primary care medical schools in the *US News & World Report* rankings increased from less than $18,000 in 1992 to more than $52,000 in 2016.[8] Given such a large expenditure, students may well expect the highest quality in all aspects of their education, including the quality of the library resources and services.

Changes in Clinical Care

In addition to evolving cultural and educational trends, another set of changes affecting medical libraries is found in clinical care. To achieve economies of scale and to save costs, hospitals and medical centers are getting bigger, merging, and consolidating. One example of this is the growth and expansion of the hospital served by the Yale medical library.

Melanie J. Norton and Nathan Rupp

Growth of Hospitals

Yale–New Haven Hospital (YNHH), the hospital served by the Cushing/Whitney Medical Library (CWML) at Yale University, has grown from 13 beds in the early 1800s to more than fifteen hundred beds today.[9] Along the way, it has changed locations and added a children's and cancer wing. It also has a children's wing located at Bridgeport Hospital, about a half hour away from New Haven, and employs physicians and residents at several other sites located throughout Connecticut. This has required the CWML to think strategically about the size of its clinical librarian staff, who are now being asked to work off-site assisting physicians and nurses located at one of these other locations.

Mergers and Acquisitions

The culmination of YNHH's growth was represented by its expansion in 2012 from one thousand to fifteen hundred beds through the addition of the Hospital of Saint Raphael, also located in New Haven. CWML's head of Collection Development and Management worked with the librarian at the Hospital of Saint Raphael, CWML's clinical librarian, senior CWML administrators, and vendors to plan and budget for the expansion of electronic resources access to the expanded hospital.

Different Locations

YNHH is just one hospital in a larger health system that includes four other hospitals and several medical offices located throughout Connecticut, Rhode Island, and New York. The offices include outpatient centers dealing with blood draw, oncology, occupational medicine, radiology, and urgent care. Although none of the medical libraries serving the five hospitals in the system has yet been asked to provide service at these locations, if they were at some time in the future, it would entail many adjustments in managing such a far-flung staff. These adjustments might include the coordination of meetings via videoconference, providing a way for staff members to confer with distant supervisors. Although this type of situation is not unusual for multinational corporations, it would be a unique way of operating for libraries.

Changing Role of Medical Libraries

The changes discussed above have had a major impact on medical libraries. Their role as storehouses for information has been significantly reduced, they no longer provide the only means of accessing information, and their role in training patrons in the use of some information technology has grown. These changes impel medical libraries to become creative—developing new services, reimagining the use of space, and exploring new ways to deliver content and support research.

New Library Services

The reduction of traditional services has led to the introduction of new services in libraries that would have been inconceivable a generation ago. Some examples include support for geographic information systems (GIS), scholarly communication, data management, and statistical support using software such as SPSS and SAS. Over the past twenty years, libraries have begun to view these common-good services as something they should provide to all users across the academic campus. The centralization of these services in the library benefits everyone, but requires librarians to shift focus from traditional bibliographic, instruction, and research skills to greater knowledge of statistical and GIS software as well as databases, digital repositories, and metadata to support data set creation.

Some of these new services represent opportunities for librarians to expand on expertise they already have. Researchers are increasingly asked by the foundations and granting agencies that fund them to provide access to the data used in their research so that others can attest to its reproducibility. Historically, it has been the purview of libraries to store information, create metadata from it, ensure it can be retrieved at a later date, and preserve it for use by other researchers. Libraries can bring this broad skill set to the management of many kinds of research data. In addition to maintaining bookshelves, managing the front end of a library catalog, or repairing older books, library staff members now need to manage databases, know other forms of metadata besides machine-readable cataloging (MARC), design interfaces for databases, and understand how to migrate data from one technology platform to another. The functions of research data management are the same, but the skills needed are different. The traditional skills of some staff members can be adapted for this new function, but others cannot; for example, a cataloger familiar with working with MARC may not necessarily have the coding skills for working with metadata in a non-MARC environment.

Distinction between Unique and Common Services

There has been a recognition over the last several years that departmental libraries—such as medical libraries—need to identify the unique services they can provide their patrons. Back-office services like cataloging, acquisitions, circulation, and interlibrary loan (ILL) can often be supported by the main library on campus, whose staff has developed significant levels of expertise in providing these services. Departmental libraries must determine whether to outsource these types of services to the main library or retain them because of

Melanie J. Norton and Nathan Rupp

the specialized needs of their patrons. At CWML, the research is driven more by journal literature than monograph, so it made sense to keep the library's ILL services in-house but outsource the library's monograph acquisitions processes, since so few monographs are acquired by the library for its patrons. Regardless of the decision, staff supporting back-office services that are outsourced may be redeployed to provide other services within the library.

Delivery of Electronic Content

Medical library collections now consist of more electronic than print content; the 2014-2015 Association of Academic Health Sciences Libraries (AAHSL) annual report shows that the average collections budget of AAHSL libraries that year was $2.077 million and that the average spent on electronic resources was $2.019 million. This means that the average AAHSL library spent more than 97 percent of its collections budget on electronic content.[10] The move from print to electronic content has resulted in new opportunities for medical library staff. Patrons no longer have to go to the physical library to access this content, so the connection between the library and the content it delivers can be lost. For this reason, medical libraries may need to invest in staff who can market the collection more aggressively than before so that users understand that the licensed content they find through a Google search is not actually free but is paid for by the library. Medical libraries may also need to invest in staff who can assist users with accessing this content remotely or think about staffing a help desk for longer hours to assist users not actually doing their research in the library.

Changes in Library Space

Because the trend is for libraries to no longer be used primarily as storehouses for printed information, they must seriously consider the functionality of their space. The most successful library facilities provide a mix of services within their space. Ideally, libraries will continue to afford users a quiet haven in which to reflect, think, and study; provide more support for group study and training areas; and introduce spaces to support interdisciplinary collaboration.[11] Libraries must consider how best to ensure space for these programs and provide new support for others. It is usually much easier to reimagine a library's current space then to build new space, so as use of the print collection declines, it is important for the library to determine which items can remain on-site and which can be stored off-site or removed altogether, thus freeing up space for new programs. As fewer materials are stored on-site, fewer staff will be needed to process, shelve, and maintain them. Finally, because patrons are less likely to visit the library to access printed information, the library needs to expand efforts to engage with them where they work—in labs, departments, grand rounds, and other settings beyond the physical library.

Changes in Library Support for Research

The library's monopoly over access to information has been broken. Basic tools such as reference indexes and search engines have been moved online and can be accessed remotely by anyone. The general public is much more familiar with online information searching than it was twenty years ago. More involved research questions have replaced individual, ready reference-type questions, and the library needs to think carefully about how it can leverage this expertise. Literature supports the need for medical libraries to provide research expertise to support the faculty and hospital curriculum.[12] These in-depth research services could include providing systematic reviews, embedding librarian support on research teams, or accompanying clinicians on rounds. These new services may require a staff member with a different type of educational background. Instead of the traditional liberal arts background, medical library staff may need a background in biomedical sciences. Instead of the skills needed to act as traditional reference librarians, they may need to have the skill sets to be informationists.

Former Library Activities

As medical libraries build out these new services and staffing models, they will need to discontinue others, because no library can provide every service it would like to. For example, the library may need to rethink the idea that it is a place primarily for storing or accessing the information found there. Instead of storing books on-site and hiring staff to ensure the materials can be found on the shelves, it may need to hire staff to create online tutorials showing users how to use the digital collections. This is a perfect example of the library giving up one service and introducing another.

Staffing Implications

All these changes in medical librarianship have significant implications for staffing. Opportunities may present themselves to redesign and rewrite job descriptions, redeploy staff to take on new responsibilities, retrain staff to acquire new skills, and hire new staff. In addition, medical libraries can differentiate between core and peripheral activities as well as in-house services that could be outsourced to other library units or even external organizations. Finally, special considerations need to be made for libraries operating within a union environment and for employees who are nearing the end of their careers.

Job Description Redesign

When writing job descriptions to reflect new responsibilities and mandates, managers should keep a number of things in mind. First, if a library has gone several years without a substantial reorganization or restructuring, it may

Melanie J. Norton and Nathan Rupp

be important to survey job descriptions currently on file. Finding these job descriptions may be difficult, especially if the staff members have been employed at the library for a long period of time. If this is the case, the library may want to create a new, more formal repository for them, leveraging tools and resources available from the main library or university human resources unit. Such a repository could include mechanisms for tracking revisions to job descriptions over time.

Second, it is important to write any new job descriptions within the context of requirements set by the central human resources department. If the job descriptions require approval by senior managers from across the library system, they must be written in a format that will be understood and accepted by all administrators. Third, to help support a nimble organization for the long-term, the job descriptions should be written in a flexible manner so that employees who move into these positions aren't pigeonholed into a single set of responsibilities. For example, at CWML, an acquisitions position was reclassified as a technical services assistant, meaning that employee could easily focus on acquisitions as well as other aspects of technical services, such as cataloging. Fourth, in support of a nimble organization, managers from different departments may want to collaborate on job descriptions that allow staff to work across departments. At CWML, for example, a position formerly devoted to technical services was rewritten so that the next hire into that position could also assist in access and public services. Writing the position in this way reflected the library's desire to begin building a staff that could fulfill multiple roles as the need arose.

Staff Redeployment

Once job descriptions have been updated or rewritten, several factors must be considered as managers redeploy staff into their new roles. Problems may arise between staff who now find themselves working more closely together. Spacing and equipment changes may need to be addressed as staff are moved to different departments. A systematic review process should be implemented to assess how the new staffing arrangement is working three, six, or twelve months down the road. Similarly, a staffing review process should be tied to the library's strategic planning process. This will ensure that adjustments to staffing are always in step with the overall strategic plan.

As staff are redeployed throughout the library, communication is essential. Staff should clearly know what their new duties are, what departments they are working in, and to which managers they will be reporting. This communication could include staff meetings to discuss the library's reorganization, meetings between staff reassigned to various departments, and, if the library operates within a bargaining unit, meetings with union representatives. Patrons should also be informed about the library's new services and departments, and how staff can help them in their new roles. This communication can take the form of library liaison meetings with their departments, library newsletters, and the library's website and social media presence. As important as staff redeployment is to serving the needs of the twenty-first-century medical library, it will fail unless the importance of restructuring is communicated to the library staff, to the larger library system, and to the faculty, staff, and students served by the library.

With redeployment, staff might find themselves working with colleagues they haven't worked with before. Managers may need to allow extra time for staff members to learn how to work together before any assessments are made. If friction does occur and interferes with their duties, management may need to bring in a coach from human resources to resolve the issue. As staff are redeployed, the library may need to reconfigure its physical work spaces. Furniture may need to be moved, computer equipment rearranged, phone numbers reassigned, and new signage rolled out. When a retiring clinical librarian at CWML was moved from the main reference office area to a space in technical services, it was discovered that the entryway to that department did not list the names of the staff who worked there. A nameplate was added on the door so faculty and students could find him. A library may even need to create a new map of its space and make the map available on its website to show where new and redeployed staff are located.

Staff Retraining

Managers need to examine the best methods to retrain staff. Options for training include self-directed training, classes offered by the larger library system or elsewhere on campus, online training, and even one-on-one training between staff members. A plan will be needed for the transition period between the design of the new staffing model, the training, and the actual redeployment of staff. Managers should also determine the correct amount of training needed so employees can learn new skills before they are deployed, so they can perform their new tasks in an efficient manner. During this transition period, it is important that the medical library maintain its current level of service, even as it begins to offer new services.[13] Finally, managers need to think about staff who may not quite fit into the new plan. As the library moves in new directions, some staff members may not want to give up responsibilities they have performed for years or may otherwise find it difficult—or impossible—to adapt to the new environment. Library managers should meet with these staff members to discuss how they can fit into a redesigned library or help them identify other opportunities on campus or even outside the institution.

Melanie J. Norton and Nathan Rupp

Hiring New Staff

In some cases, the new services the medical library wishes to offer will require more employee expertise than a series of webinars and workshops can provide. In these cases, the medical library may need to hire new staff who already have the required skill sets or expertise. In order to do this, the administration may need to make the case with its funders (the main library system, hospital, and/or medical school) that the new position is needed. They must then work with the human resources department to initiate a search to fill the new position and take care to go about this process the right way. It is important for managers to create a series of interview questions to ascertain whether a candidate has the right professional qualifications and background for the job and is the best fit for the library's culture.

Onboarding is a critical part of the hiring process. For example, approximately three years ago, CWML found it needed to expand services in support of bioinformatics data. There were no staff available who could support this expansion, so the library made the case for, and then hired, its first bioinformatics librarian. This new hire had a background in biology, including work in a genetics laboratory. Other areas of expertise that medical libraries might need to hire for include support for GIS, data management, and research design. Employees with degrees in these disciplines may command higher salaries than libraries are used to paying, so they need to be prepared to have this discussion when approaching their funders. These special staff hires may represent opportunities for collaboration with other library units across campus, or even other units within the schools or other organizations supported by the library. These departments or organizations may also need an expert in GIS or bioinformatics, for example, and the higher salary could be shared between the departments or organizations. However, the two would need to work closely together to set up a schedule governing where the subject expert would be working throughout the course of the week, then take care to review the schedule and larger job-sharing arrangement on a periodic basis.

Outsourcing Services

In addition to sharing staff expertise across campus, the library may also identify services and activities that can be completely outsourced to another library, another unit on campus, or an external vendor. These could be services that no longer make sense to do in-house, or they could be new services that would be best supported by other libraries or units on campus. Specifically, there is often a desire on the part of the library to outsource back-office activities and services, including technical services operations such as acquisitions, cataloging, electronic resources management, and preservation, as well as access services operations such as interlibrary loan. For example, CWML recently outsourced the acquisition and processing of non-rare print materials to the main library on campus, freeing up a staff member to provide support for the Research and Education Department, including work at the library's public services desks.

Libraries considering this type of outsourcing need to be careful to ensure that their requirements can be met by the external organization. The external organization may have workflows that are significantly different from those historically maintained by the medical library, so the medical library needs to determine whether it can live with workflow changes. Again, CWML is a good example: although the main library at Yale maintains an interlibrary loan unit that could have absorbed the medical library's ILL, the medical library administration felt that because medical research is very time sensitive, this process needed to be retained in-house. Finally, any library outsourcing its work to another library unit, another division within the parent organization, or an outside vendor needs to establish a timetable to assess this work on a periodic basis.

Working in a Union Environment

Institutions operating within a union environment need to take special care when making any type of staff changes. Institutions with unions need to be aware of the current union contract, rules, and procedures before making any changes to staff job descriptions. It is very important to involve union representatives at every step of the reorganization process so that employees resistant to change know about their options within the context of the union contract. For example, if the library were to eliminate a position, the employee may be able to take advantage of the union pool of employees who are able to apply first for any other open unionized positions on campus. The union contract may specifically require employee participation meetings that allow employees to learn about the upcoming changes to the library and how these changes will affect them. Communication with the union representative should begin very early in the process so the bargaining unit understands the needs of the library and the reasons for the reorganizational process.

End-of-Career Employees

Special care needs to be taken when incorporating employees nearing the end of their career into any new comprehensive staffing plan. These senior employees may not see the need to change their skills, and the library may not want to devote much time to retraining or adding skills if an employee plans to retire in six months to a year. Instead, managers need to identify which skills and responsibilities senior employees can retain, which they can give up, and what new responsibilities they can assume. A librarian skilled at

Melanie J. Norton and Nathan Rupp

liaison work and outreach to departments and individual faculty members should be encouraged to continue that work, even if the types of questions he or she is answering have changed and require a different skill set (data management instead of literature review questions, for example). He or she could be partnered with a newer librarian for introduction to department heads and individual faculty members. Senior librarians could be encouraged to be formal mentors to younger librarians—introducing them to the new workplace and its culture. Finally, libraries need to ensure that the institutional knowledge held by senior librarians is transmitted to younger librarians before the former retires. In some cases, there may be a very good reason a job has been done a particular way; sometimes "we've always done it that way" is the correct way. Libraries need to find ways to involve employees who are nearing retirement even if the library undergoes reorganization or embraces other major changes.

Conclusion

Over the last quarter century, a number of changes have taken place that affect all libraries, and specifically medical libraries—changes that involve the types of services they provide, the methods they use to deliver those services, and the patron base to which they deliver those services. As these aspects of the medical library change, its staff also needs to change. This chapter has provided examples of the types of changes experienced by medical libraries, how they have affected library services, and some of the staffing changes that should be considered. The following chapters will provide more specific discussion about some of the staffing implications that medical libraries will need to consider in the twenty-first century.

Notes

1. F. Manjoo, "Think Amazon's Drone Delivery Is a Gimmick? Think Again," *New York Times,* August 10, 2016, accessed August 14, 2017, https://www.nytimes.com/2016/08/11/technology/think-amazons-drone-delivery-idea-is-a-gimmick-think-again.html.
2. Pew Research Center, "Fewer Than Half of U.S. Kids Today Live in a 'Traditional Family,'" 2014, accessed March 24, 2017, http://www.pewresearch.org/fact-tank/2014/12/22/less-than-half-of-u-s-kids-today-live-in-a-traditional-family.
3. Ibid.
4. Pew Research Center, "The Rise in Dual Income Households," 2015, accessed March 24, 2017, http://www.pewresearch.org/ft_dual-income-households-1960-2012-2.
5. US Youth Soccer, "Key Statistics: Membership Statistics," 2012, accessed March 24, 2017, http://www.usyouthsoccer.org/media_kit/keystatistics.
6. Central Michigan University, "Global Campus," accessed April 4, 2017, https://www.cmich.edu/Global/Pages/default.aspx.
7. Liaison Committee on Medical Education, (2017). "Accredited MD Programs in the United States," 2017, accessed April 4, 2017, http://lcme.org/directory/accredited-u-s-programs.

8. "The Best Graduate Schools: Medicine," *US News & World Report*, 112, no 11 (March 23, 1992): 88–89; *US News & World Report*, "2017 Best Medical Schools," accessed July 18, 2016, http://grad-schools.usnews.rankingsandreviews.com/best-graduate-schools/top-medical-schools.
9. Yale New Haven Health/Yale New Haven Hospital, "History and Heritage," accessed April 25, 2017, https://www.ynhh.org/about/hospital-overview/history-heritage .aspx.
10. S. J. Squires et al., eds. *Annual Statistics of Medical School Libraries in the United States and Canada*, 38th ed. (Seattle: Association of Academic Health Sciences Libraries, 2016).
11. D. A. Lindberg and B. L. Humphreys, "2015—The Future of Medical Libraries," *New England Journal of Medicine* 352, no. 11 (March 17, 2005): 1067–70.
12. D. W. Lewis, "A Strategy for Academic Libraries in the First Quarter of the 21st Century," *College & Research Libraries* 68, no. 5 (2007): 418–34.
13. M. Henderson, "New Roles and new Horizons for Health Sciences Librarians and Libraries," in *Health Sciences Librarianship*, ed. M. S. Wood (Chicago: Rowman & Littlefield, 2014), 405–20.

Chapter 2

Empowering Staff

Teresa L. Knott

Employee empowerment literature is abundant. While there is a small body of literature on empowerment in library environments, little is written about empowerment in health sciences libraries. However, empowerment based in other sectors—such as government, health-care systems, hospitals, higher education, or nonprofits—can be highly relevant.

In most organizations, the greatest assets are human resources. Employees have the power to drive organizational success and are typically one of the largest items budgeted. Although found in the literature earlier, employee empowerment emerged as a management concept and tool in the late 1980s as companies began to implement employee empowerment programs.

Over time, two fundamental approaches emerged to define employee empowerment: structural and psychological. Structural or managerial empowerment is essentially delegated authority, or how managers share authority and power with staff. It encompasses organizational policies and practices that grant employees more discretion and influence on how they perform their work. Psychological empowerment is based on a motivational construct that focuses on intrinsic task motivation and improving feelings of self-efficacy in internal cognition. It focuses on employees' perceptions and cognition.[1] Psychological empowerment is widely agreed to involve four elements: meaning, competence, self-determination, and impact.[2] For group empowerment, B. L. Kirkman and B. Rosen translate this to the meaningfulness of the work, the perceived ability to solve the task at hand, the perceived autonomy to accomplish a job, and the perceived impact of what a work unit does.[3]

In 2012, S. Fernandez and T. Moldogaziev noted that "empowerment might best be understood as a *process* involving a set of management practices (sharing authority, resources, information, and rewards) that influence performance (effort, productivity) not only directly but also indirectly through their impact on employee cognition (self-efficacy, motivation and job satisfaction)."[4] K. W. Thomas and B. A. Velthouse note that *empower* means "to give power to" and that power can be considered energy. Thus, *empowerment* can mean "to energize," which may better capture the motivational use of the term.[5] Empowerment can be examined from an individual or group perspective.

Why empower? According to G. A. Yukl and W. S. Becker, empowerment initiatives should be twofold. The objectives should be to improve organizational effectiveness and to improve the quality of life for employees.[6] In the public sector, empowerment is viewed as a means to improve the quality of public services and to unleash the creative abilities of public employees. In Fernandez and Moldogaziev's review of the literature, empowerment gives employees the flexibility and resources to address customer needs; increases concentration, effort, and resilience because of high task motivation; increases job satisfaction and commitment through sharing power, resources, and knowledge; improves individual productivity and effectiveness; improves the quality of interactions with customers; and promotes innovativeness.[7]

Individual Empowerment

Based on G. M. Spreitzer's construct, all four elements—*meaningfulness, competence, autonomy*, and *impact*—must be present to achieve individual empowerment. In addition, there are four antecedents to psychological empowerment. The first is self-esteem. Employees with *self-esteem* believe they have knowledge, skills, and talents to contribute to an organization. Employees with strong self-esteem are more likely to be proactive, while employees with weak self-esteem do not perceive an ability to actively impact their working environment.[8]

The second antecedent is *locus of control*. In 1966, J. B. Rotter suggested that locus of control is a measure of the degree to which an individual believes external forces determine what happens in their lives. Individuals with a positive locus of control believe they can influence their environment.[9] Library employees with a positive locus of control believe they can more actively shape their working environment.

Other antecedents to empowerment are *information* and *rewards*. Information—such as the library's mission, vision, and values—can create a strong sense of purpose within the staff. This information gives staff a framework through which to assess and do their work. Information about individual performance can influence decision making and future performance, and can reinforce perceptions of competency. Systems of rewards recognize contributions and may provide incentives for better performance and contributions to decision making.[10]

Meaningfulness

When assessing empowerment, meaningfulness is based on the value, worth, or importance of a specific task or project being done. It is based on an individual's values and ideals. Individual values and ideals are the lens through which a person assesses the meaningfulness of her work. It has to answer the questions, "Does it matter to me or to my unit?" and "Do I care about this task?" Low levels of meaningfulness are associated with apathy, while higher levels of meaningfulness are associated with engagement and commitment.[11]

For practical purposes, health sciences libraries have an innate advantage when it comes to the concept of meaningfulness. By their very nature, libraries are organizations that serve the public good. With the focus on health, clinical care, educating health professionals, and facilitating research and discovery, health sciences libraries and their staff contribute to the greater good. This should serve as an excellent foundation for addressing the empowerment element of meaning for library staff at every level. A library's mission, vision, and values should provide a framework for staff to relate the impact of their job.

One of the most powerful tools a leader possesses is the ability to connect vision to action or to imbue work with meaningfulness. This can occur by tying individual performance standards and goals to the organization's mission, vision, and values. It can be challenging and time consuming to work with staff to make this connection, but it can result in a deeper commitment to doing the best job possible. For instance, a classified staff member who works in interlibrary loan may feel as if he or she is just a cog in the wheel who receives, handles, and fills requests for material, and may be challenged to glean the impact of his or her position. He or she may routinely have direct interactions with service users, but generally feels that he or she is just processing an endless stream of requests. Engaging in a conversation with a manager about the tremendous impact of delivering articles to a clinician trying to address treatment challenges with a child with a rare condition or to a researcher who is working on a multiyear grant to investigate this rare condition may help the staff member better grasp how he or she personally contributes to higher organizational goals. In this case, meaning can be enhanced by connecting the items retrieved to the organization's mission, which is typically centered on teaching, research, and clinical care. Explaining the impact of a single article on the outcome for a patient can engender a deeper connection to the overall purpose of the job for the staff member.

Competence

According to Thomas and Velthouse, competence "refers to the degree to which a person can perform task activities skillfully when he or she tries."[12] This is an area that may be the easiest for a manager to address through training, feedback, and mentoring. Using data from the 2006 Federal Human Capital Survey (FHCS), conducted by the US Office of Personnel Management, Fernandez and Moldogaziev found evidence that providing employees with opportunities to learn and enhance their skills and knowledge improved their effectiveness and encouraged innovation.[13] In presenting additional results of their study on the 2006 FHCS, Fernandez and Moldogaziev determined that "offering employees opportunities to gain job-related knowledge and skills has the largest substantive effect on perceptions of performance."[14] Highly skilled employees are better able to diagnosis problems and implement solutions.

Referencing the work of Russ Forrester, Yukl and Becker note that organizations that "invest in building employee skills, achievement orientation, and self confidence can increase the likelihood of successful empowerment."[15] As learning organizations, health sciences libraries should consistently offer employees opportunities to gain new skills and knowledge. A health sciences reference librarian in 1980 needed excellent database-searching skills. In many academic health sciences centers, that need transformed into a requirement that a liaison librarian have an in-depth understanding of searching skills across many databases and the gray literature to support systematic reviews of the literature as well as the need to understand levels of evidence related to clinical practice. As health sciences libraries moved to a single service point, classified staff members were called upon to learn more about providing basic reference services. These changes require an ongoing investment in training and employee development to produce more knowledgeable and effective employees.

Cross-training can be an effective employee empowerment tool. By training employees to do tasks typically performed by a colleague, a manager can build confidence in individual staff members and make them feel they are valuable to the organization. Cross-training builds flexibility for the organization should an employee leave. It increases knowledge of work processes and fosters a fresh look at processes that may result in suggestions for improvement or new

Teresa L. Knott

approaches to problem solving. Employees who are more knowledgeable about how an organization functions may be more confident in making decisions and recommending improvements.[16] K. Greasley wrote, "[I]t's like a circle, the more confident you are the more decisions you make."[17]

Managers can reinforce feelings of competence through both positive feedback and annual assessment processes. Being acknowledged for good work makes an employee feel more capable and thus empowered. Competency can be seen as building blocks, where employees are given training and increasingly more complex tasks to perform. In his 1986 text, A. Bandura states, "People who are persuaded verbally that they possess the capabilities to master given tasks are likely to mobilize greater sustained effort than if they harbor self-doubts and dwell on personal deficiencies when difficulties arise."[18]

Autonomy

Autonomy or choice is based on the individual's perceived level of self-determination. Autonomy is the degree to which employees decide how they will work.[19] In our complex organizations, an employee may be given a great deal of autonomy in one area of responsibility, while another area of responsibility may be more structured. Autonomy can be as simple as giving an employee the option of how and when tasks are completed. It can be negotiating a desired outcome with an employee and allowing the employee the freedom to decide how he or she will accomplish the agreed-upon outcome.

A classified staff member's day may be structured around time scheduled on a service desk, but he or she may have the freedom to complete the rest of his or her daily assignments in the order he or she prefers. For a liaison librarian, autonomy can be deciding the most appropriate methods for reaching out to an assigned program or creating a new workshop that meets a niche need for nursing students, such as searching drug resources.

Impact

Impact is the degree to which an individual's task performance or behavior can "make a difference." Does the individual believe that his or her behavior or performance accomplish the purpose of the task, producing the intended effect? This element of empowerment is focused on an individual's belief that he or she can perform the task competently and deliver the preferred outcome. It is not based on effort.[20] An individual has impact in his or her position when he or she believes that he or she can influence outcomes at work, whether those outcomes are operational, administrative, or strategic. The opposite of impact is learned helplessness.[21]

A librarian who serves as the liaison to a pharmacy school is likely to persist in building relationships with faculty when he or she perceives that his or her work impacts faculty research and student success. Impact may become apparent when a faculty member refers a colleague or when a fourth-year student in an experiential rotation thanks him or her for his or her assistance. A supervisor can encourage this librarian to consider his or her impact by routinely asking the liaison to share his or her work and success stories.

Team Empowerment

In the twenty-first century, there has been a growth in matrix organizations and the use of teams to achieve work in hospitals and academic medical centers. When they examined team empowerment, Kirkman and Rosen posited that team empowerment could be assessed using four dimensions: *potency*, *meaningfulness*, *autonomy*, and *impact*. These are based on elements of individual empowerment, with potency substituting for competence. Team meaningfulness, autonomy, and impact are roughly equivalent to individual elements but are based on a team perspective. For instance, meaningfulness is a measure of how a team perceives its task as valuable. Team members can influence the experience of meaningfulness for each other.[22] Table 2.1 compares the elements of individual and team empowerment.

For a team, autonomy is the degree to which team members experience discretion or independence in their work. Kirkman and Rosen explained that high levels of team autonomy may decrease individual autonomy because decision making is shared. Like individual impact, team impact occurs when a team produces significant work for the organization.[23]

Table 2.1. Elements of Individual and Team Empowerment

Individual Empowerment	Individual Empowerment	Team Empowerment
Thomas & Velthouse	Voegtlin	Kirkman & Rosen
Impact	Impact	Impact
Meaningfulness	Meaningfulness	Meaningfulness
Choice	Perceived Autonomy	Autonomy
Competence	Perceived Power	Potency

K. W. Thomas and B. A. Velthouse, "Cognitive Elements of Empowerment: An 'Interpretive' Model of Intrinsic Task Motivation," *Academy of Management Review* 15, no. 4 (1990): 666–81; C. Voegtlin, S. A. Boehm, and H. Bruch, "How to Empower Employees: Using Training to Enhance Work Units' Collective Empowerment," *International Journal of Manpower* 36, no. 3 (2015): 354–73; B. L. Kirkman and B. Rosen, "Beyond Self-Management: Antecedents and Consequences of Team Empowerment," *Academy of Management Journal* 42, no. 1 (1999): 58–74.

Teresa L. Knott

Team potency is different from individual competence or self-efficacy in three ways: (1) potency refers to team performance while self-efficacy refers to individual performance; (2) potency experiences develop collectively while self-efficacy experiences are personal and private; and (3) potency refers to general effectiveness while self-efficacy refers to performance of specific tasks.[24]

In their field study of the dimensions of team empowerment, Kirkman and Rosen determined that "team empowerment was significantly related to external team leader behaviors, production/service responsibilities, team-based human resources policies, and social structures." They also determined that team empowerment was "significantly related to productivity, customer service, job satisfaction, organizational commitment, and team commitment." They concluded that "team empowerment was positively associated with a broad range of positive employee and organizational outcomes such as commitment, proactivity, and customer service."[25]

Managers can act to empower teams at different levels of the organization by: (1) ensuring that team leaders are trained to exhibit appropriate behavior and to act as role models for their teams by encouraging teams to set high standards and to solve their problems; (2) allowing team members to participate in goal setting and taking responsibility for their area or solving assigned problems; and (3) changing social structures to increase team access to information and resources and to build communication and coordination.[26]

Team-building endeavors can impact the effectiveness of the organization, as can skill or knowledge building. One library developed a team-based training program by pairing a classified staff member with a faculty member to explore and team-teach colleagues about lesser-used licensed databases. The purpose of the exercise was threefold: break down barriers between classified staff and librarians, improve knowledge about individual databases, and improve awareness across the staff about databases with relevant content.

Structural Empowerment

Structural empowerment is based on delegated authority, or how a manager shares power and authority with staff members. It essentially moves decision making down the organizational hierarchy.[27] Managers need to understand employees who report to them and have a good understanding of their capabilities before delegating tasks. A manager should consider the level of interest an employee may have in a task or project. If an employee is a whiz at spreadsheets, assigning a project that heavily relies on extrapolating data from spreadsheets may be appropriate; however, if an employee has little to no skill with spreadsheets, this would not be an appropriate delegation without a plan to invest in improving the employee's skill level.

An important component of structural empowerment is *information sharing*. To act responsibly, employees need access to relevant information about the task or the project. Shared information reduces uncertainty and fosters empowered behavior.[28] Delegated tasks should meet certain parameters. If authority is delegated, relevant information, boundaries, and reporting requirements should be outlined in advance. If a task is not central to the manager's role, it can be delegated. Appropriate tasks—pleasant and unpleasant—should be delegated.

Delegated tasks should be relevant to the employee's work and have clearly defined outcomes. For instance, a circulation employee may be empowered to waive fines up to twenty-five dollars, with supervisor approval required beyond that amount. Appropriate coworkers should be informed of the employee's newly delegated responsibilities. For tasks, the manager should continue to check in with the employee to see if he or she needs additional information or support and how he or she is progressing toward accomplishing the task. Ideally, delegated tasks become learning opportunities. Managers should also remember that some of the best learning opportunities come from making mistakes. Empowerment fails in a culture of mistake avoidance.[29]

Organizational Culture

Yukl and Becker defined organizational culture as "shared values, beliefs, and norms held by members of an organization." They noted that a culture that strongly values information sharing, fair and constructive judgment of ideas, and reward and recognition for new ideas leads to creative problem solving.[30]

Creating a culture or an environment of empowerment for staff is a purposeful act that requires ongoing attention. A central component of empowering staff is that staff members believe their manager or leader is trustworthy. *Trust* is built on predictability and meeting expectations. A leader can build a framework of trust by clearly laying out expectations and by specifying where and how staff members have latitude. The framework can be built with policies and procedures, but it must also reflect opportunities for staff to exercise creativity and judgment.

Trust

At a macro level, S. H. Appelbaum asserts that "a team based structure and a culture based on trust and open communication are the key factors affecting the successful implementation of empowerment."[31] M. J. Moye and A. B. Henkin note that "trust reinforces the effectiveness of the decision-making processes,

Teresa L. Knott

is an important factor in terms of employee willingness to collaborate, and strengthens employee capacity to handle crises."[32]

Trust between individuals is significant for the stability and success of an organization. It can impact employee well-being. It is strongly associated with performance, quality of communication, risk taking, problem solving, and cooperation. It is necessary for cooperation and collaboration within an organization. Among other things, trust is based on competence, dependability, responsibility, and reliability. For Moye and Henkin's research, interpersonal trust was defined as the "extent to which an employee is confident in, and willing to act on the basis of the words, actions, and decisions of his or her manager/supervisor."[33] Managers can strengthen relational trust by being trustworthy. Trustworthiness can be demonstrated through consistency, caring, integrity, communication, and concern for employees. In 1977, R. M. Steers found that when employees perceive that their organization keeps commitments it makes, employees are more likely to be committed in turn.[34]

Communication

Intertwined with trust is *communication*. The most trusted managers communicate clearly and accurately.[35] Sharing information can raise the level of trust between employee and manager.[36] Additionally, leaders and managers are role models for setting appropriate goals, valuing individual contributions, and showing confidence in staff members.[37] They should be able to clearly and powerfully articulate the mission, vision, and values of the parent organization and the library in ways that are meaningful to employees.

An essential act of communication in a supervisory relationship is that of setting achievable performance goals and clearly defining expectations for behavior and performance. Performance goals should be negotiated between the employee and supervisor. Good managers routinely solicit feedback from and provide feedback to staff members. Managers should strive to be strong active listeners to enhance this feedback loop. Beyond the performance cycle, managers should also solicit feedback from staff members who are less likely to express concerns or opinions. In return, managers should avoid becoming defensive when staff members are sharing opinions and perspectives that might make the manager uncomfortable.[38]

In 1995, D. E. Bowen and E. E. Lawler III noted that "many empowerment programs fail when they focus on 'power' without also redistributing information, knowledge, and rewards."[39] Information about the status of the library and its parent organization is vital knowledge for staff members. As an example, if the library is part of a state-funded university and the local newspaper is publishing stories about state budget cuts, staff members are more likely to feel empowered and secure if library leaders have communicated the organization's plans for handling budget cuts.

To support empowerment for teams and to move employees toward self-direction, J. R. Schultz suggests that managers should communicate to:

- Ensure that their work has a clear purpose with well-defined expected results.
- Ensure that staff has the skills and knowledge to perform the desired work through training.
- Allow those doing the work and their informal leaders the responsibility to establish the details of how work is accomplished.
- Not reverse team decisions without consulting team members and gaining their consent.
- Provide a process for addressing injustices and the political power to deal with internal or external power structures that might interfere with the team's ability to freely engage in their assigned activity.[40]

As with many elements of staff empowerment, communication is a broad topic with a tremendous body of literature that is worth delving into in a more comprehensive manner.

Transparency

Linked to trust and communication is the concept of *transparency*. Organizational and managerial transparency can reinforce a climate of trust and empowerment for employees. Transparency at one level might be engaging staff throughout the organization in a strategic planning process. Asking staff at all levels to participate in a SWOT (strengths, weaknesses, opportunities, threats) analysis or an environmental scan can produce more robust results, since each person has a different perspective of the organization and different interactions with internal and external constituencies. If it is not feasible to engage every employee, it is useful to get periodic feedback as planning proceeds.

Rewards

There are many ways to reward empowered employees who deliver excellence. In some instances, it may be possible to recognize excellence through financial incentives tied to achieving specific goals. If an organization is able to provide financial incentives for performance to individuals or teams, the parameters for rewards should be outlined in advance and be freely available for all eligible employees to review. In some organizations, employees might be rewarded with time off not charged to their leave balances.

Teresa L. Knott

In organizations where it is not possible to recognize outstanding performance financially or through leave, managers may opt to use more creative mechanisms. Successful, empowered employees can be recognized publicly or privately. Recognition should always begin with a manager specifically expressing appreciation for what the employee did that was excellent and thanking the employee for his or her work with an explanation of the difference the employee's or team's actions made for the manager, the unit, or the organization. Individual or team success can be recognized at periodic meetings.

Celebrating successful or project completion within the health sciences library can empower individuals across the organization, and it can also foster teamwork. Staff recruitment, retention, and rewards will be covered more in depth in a subsequent chapter.

Limits to Empowerment

Greasley et al. used a qualitative approach to explore the limits to empowerment. In their 2007 article, they found that employees did not recognize and ascribe meaning to the term *empowerment*. However, employees were able to describe key concepts related to empowerment. Employees in the study cohort clearly believed team leaders and supervisors should accept greater responsibility and serve as a buffer to protect employees. Doing so enabled employees to focus on their own work rather than on issues that were beyond their control. Greasley et al. learned that some employees did not want more responsibility, while others welcomed the opportunity to acquire new skills and knowledge and to be more deeply involved in projects.[41]

Employees were clear that: (1) when a decision or action involved significant financial implications for the organization, managers should make these decisions; (2) managers or experts should make decisions or solve problems that require specialized knowledge; (3) individual employees should make decisions or solve problems only at a level at which they feel competent and confident; and (4) individuals should not be called on to make managerial decisions without appropriate compensation. There was a general sentiment that managers and team leaders need to accept their responsibility to the team and should not exploit team members. Essentially, employees "are only willing to accept empowerment up to their level of capability."[42]

In 2006, Yukl and Becker concluded that empowerment initiatives failed for three reasons. First, empowerment represents change. Because empowerment represents relinquishing some control to employees, a manager may fear the loss of control and command with this change. Second, because empowerment is an ongoing process, it takes time. A one-day workshop on empowerment will not move an organization's dynamic. Growing involvement and sharing decision making are gradual processes. Last, as noted above, employees may resist empowerment endeavors. Being given more responsibility and/or freedom may induce fear and uncertainty in some employees. Some may be interested only in coming to work, doing their jobs as usual, and leaving at the end of the day. To be successful in the long term, senior leadership needs to openly support empowerment efforts, invest time, and cede some control to employees.[43]

P. Kizilos offered a cautionary reflection on empowerment when he wrote:

[M]any companies are attracted by a fantasy version of empowerment and simultaneously repelled by the reality. How lovely to have energetic, dedicated workers who always seize the initiative (but only when "appropriate"), who enjoy taking risk (but never risky ones), who volunteer their ideas (but only brilliant ones), who solve problems on their own (but make no mistakes), who aren't afraid to speak their minds (but never ruffle any feathers), who always give their best to the company (but ask not unpleasant questions about what the company is giving them back). How nice it would be, in short, to empower workers without giving them any power.[44]

Conclusion

Employee empowerment is a large, complex topic with many variables. It continues to be the subject of ongoing research. There is an enormous body of written research that the reader is encouraged to explore for a deeper understanding of the topic. Every employee is an individual with a different spectrum of behaviors and actions that he or she will find empowering.[45]

Subsequent chapters in this book explore topics that are related to or can impact employee empowerment: education and training; communication; recruitment, retention, and rewards; and organizational vision.

Quoting W. Alan Randolph, Appelbaum wrote that "managers can more easily assume their new empowering roles as coach, mentor and team leader." He goes on to explain that as a team becomes more autonomous, a manager should slowly transfer more control to the team.[46] To do this effectively, leaders and managers need to continue learning and growing in their roles. In their 2013 article, Fernandez and Moldogaziev found that "the effect of employee empowerment on job satisfaction is positive and even stronger than empowerment's direct effect of performance."[47] Increasing job satisfaction and using empowerment practices can result in improved performance. Over time, empowerment practices stimulate innovation.[48] Employee empowerment is an ongoing process, and it is a worthy investment for library organizations.

Notes

1. K. Greasley et al., "Understanding Empowerment from an Employee Perspective: What Does It Mean and Do They Want It?" *Team Performance Management* 14, no. 1 (2008): 39-55; S. Fernandez and T. Moldogaziev, "Empowering Public Sector Employees to Improve Performance: Does It Work?" *American Review of Public Administration* 41, no. 1 (2011): 23-47.
2. G. M. Spreitzer, "Psychological Empowerment in the Workplace: Dimensions, Measurement and Validation" *Academy of Management Journal* 38, no. 5 (1995): 1442-65.
3. C. Voegtlin, S. A. Boehm, and H. Bruch, "How to Empower Employees: Using Training to Enhance Work Units' Collective Empowerment," *International Journal of Manpower* 36, no. 3 (2015): 354-73.
4. S. Fernandez and T. Moldogaziev, "Using Employee Empowerment to Encourage Innovative Behavior in the Public Sector," *Journal of Public Administration Research & Theory* 23, no. 1 (2013): 157.
5. K. W. Thomas and B. A. Velthouse, "Cognitive Elements of Empowerment: An 'Interpretive' Model of Intrinsic Task Motivation," *Academy of Management Review* 15, no. 4 (1990): 667.
6. G. A. Yukl and W. S. Becker, "Effective Empowerment in Organizations," *Organization Management Journal* 3, no. 3 (2006): 210-31.
7. Fernandez and Moldogaziev, "Empowering Public Sector Employees to Improve Performance," 23-47.
8. Spreitzer, "Psychological Empowerment in the Workplace," 1442-65.
9. Ibid.
10. Ibid.
11. Thomas and Velthouse, "Cognitive Elements of Empowerment," 666-81.
12. Ibid., 672.
13. Fernandez and Moldogaziev, "Using Employee Empowerment to Encourage Innovative Behavior in the Public Sector," 155-87.
14. Fernandez and Moldogaziev, "Empowering Public Sector Employees to Improve Performance," 23-47.
15. Yukl and Becker, "Effective Empowerment in Organizations," 214.
16. Ibid.
17. Greasley et al., "Understanding Empowerment from an Employee Perspective," 46.
18. J. A. Conger and R. N. Kanungo, (1988). "The Empowerment Process: Integrating Theory and Practice," *Academy of Management Review* 13, no. 3 (1988): 479.
19. Yukl and Becker, "Effective Empowerment in Organizations," 210-31.
20. Thomas and Velthouse, "Cognitive Elements of Empowerment," 666-81.
21. Spreitzer, "Psychological Empowerment in the Workplace," 1442-65.
22. B. L. Kirkman and B. Rosen, "Beyond Self-Management: Antecedents and Consequences of Team Empowerment," *Academy of Management Journal* 42, no. 1 (1999): 58-74.
23. Ibid.
24. Ibid.

25. Ibid., 70.
26. Ibid.
27. Yukl and Becker, "Effective Empowerment in Organizations," 210-31.
28. S. H. Appelbaum et al., "Employee Empowerment: Factors Affecting the Consequent Success or Failure (Part I)," *Industrial & Commercial Training* 46, no. 7 (2014): 379-86.
29. Yukl and Becker, "Effective Empowerment in Organizations," 210-31.
30. Ibid., 214.
31. S. H. Appelbaum et al., "Employee Empowerment: Factors Affecting the Consequent Success or Failure (Part II)," *Industrial & Commercial Training* 47, no. 1 (2015): 27.
32. M. J. Moye and A. B. Henkin, "Exploring Associations between Employee Empowerment and Interpersonal Trust in Managers," *Journal of Management Development* 25, no. 2 (2006): 101.
33. Ibid., 103.
34. Kirkman and Rosen, "Beyond Self-Management," 58-74.
35. Moye and Henkin, "Exploring Associations between Employee Empowerment and Interpersonal Trust in Managers," 101-17.
36. Appelbaum et al., "Employee Empowerment (Part I)," 379-86.
37. Yukl and Becker, "Effective Empowerment in Organizations," 210-31.
38. Ibid.
39. D. E. Bowen and E. E. Lawler III, "Empowering Service Employees," *Sloan Management Review* 36, no. 4 (1995): 74.
40. J. R. Schultz, "Creating a Culture of Empowerment Fosters the Flexibility to Change," *Global Business & Organizational Excellence* 34, no. 1 (2014): 45.
41. Greasley et al., "Understanding Empowerment from an Employee Perspective," 39-55.
42. Ibid., 49.
43. Yukl and Becker, "Effective Empowerment in Organizations," 210-31.
44. P. Kizilos, "Crazy about Empowerment?" *Training* 27, no. 12 (1990): 55-56.
45. Yukl and Becker, "Effective Empowerment in Organizations," 210-31.
46. Appelbaum et al., "Employee Empowerment (Part I)," 381.
47. S. Fernandez and T. Moldogaziev, "Employee Empowerment, Employee Attitudes, and Performance: Testing a Causal Model," *Public Administration Review* 73, no. 3 (2013): 500.
48. Fernandez and Moldogaziev, "Using Employee Empowerment to Encourage Innovative Behavior in the Public Sector," 155-87.

Teresa L. Knott

Chapter 3

Skilling Up

Amy Blevins, Ryan Harris, and Elizabeth Kiscaden

Over the past twenty years, there has been a major change in how library services are offered and the work in which support staff are involved. Jo Webb gives good examples of these changes:

> Qualified librarians have moved away from direct customer contact, so that support staff do most lending and enquiry work. IT and computing staff are replacing systems specialists, and much of the work in cataloging and acquisition sections has been simplified, streamlined and automated, reducing the need for qualified staff input. Even in the traditional domain like lending services, the introduction of self-issue is changing the nature of work for all involved.[1]

Librarians identified that their work at the reference desk is less important in terms of their job duties and that focus has shifted to outreach and instruction. In turn, it has become the work of library support personnel to staff reference desks and answer questions.[2] This focus on outreach and instruction from librarians coincides with institutions examining how they offer services in their library. Many libraries have transitioned to a single service desk model that relies primarily on support staff to provide assistance. If needed, support staff will refer patrons to librarians for more in-depth support and assistance.[3] This evolution speaks to the changing roles library support staff are experiencing in their day-to-day work.

The job duties of library support staff have altered drastically. According to the Association of Academic Health Science Libraries (AAHSL) statistics for the last seven years, most libraries have seen a dramatic drop in the circulation of physical materials as libraries have transitioned to electronic materials. Many libraries have seen a drop in reference transactions as well.[4] In most cases, support staff positions are not eliminated from the library, but staff are instead developed and retained.[5] These changes underscore a need to develop support staff and utilize these talented individuals in a new and meaningful way within libraries.

M. Kent Mayfield discussed the great changes that were coming to libraries and stressed the need to discuss professional competencies in terms of four characteristics: *context, knowledge and analysis* (the ability to apply theory to real life situations), *interdependence with professional values*, and *holism*. Mayfield also says that "competence is holistic" and goes on to stress that training and professional development in the workplace should assist library staff with growing their professional identity, which is done through "the integration of knowledge, skills, personal strengths, and propensities into a coherent whole. Professional learning, then, should incorporate processes for nurturing personal strengths and potentials for working through problems."[6]

In this chapter, context sets the stage for all learning initiatives, whether they be training or professional development. As information science professionals, we have an obligation to create a culture of lifelong learning. This is a theme that emerges explicitly in articles that discuss the creation of professional development and training opportunities for library employees.[7]

Definitions

Professional learning can be broken down into two categories: professional development and training. The *Economic Times* defines *professional development* as including "all types of learning opportunities like academic degrees, conferences, and non-formal learning opportunities."[8] Merriam-Webster defines *training* as "a process by which someone is taught the skills that are needed for an art, profession, or job."[9] Training differs from professional development in that it is more task driven than philosophy driven. For example, learning how to best utilize a new integrated library system would be training, whereas learning the theories behind evidence-based medicine would likely fall under professional development. There are several different ways to ensure that library staff have the skills needed to handle new processes and resources.

Barriers and Challenges

There is a great deal of research available on professional learning across professions, and a common theme emerges with regard to barriers to successfully meeting development goals. The three primary barriers identified are:

Amy Blevins, Ryan Harris, and Elizabeth Kiscaden

- limited time to pursue professional development opportunities; the library does not provide time to pursue these opportunities;
- staff development is not a key initiative at the institution; as a result, there are limited or no resources for professional development; and
- the staff member's own perception that there is no need to pursue development opportunities.

There is a perception that as jobs become more automated, library employees will have more time, not less. In reality, duties are shifted and the workforce of library employees is reduced through attrition, leaving many employees with larger workloads that they had previously. It's a common complaint: there's too much to do and not enough time to get it all done. Ideally, time for training and professional development will be built into the workday, with release time for library employees to attend on-site opportunities, conferences, workshops, and even webinars. One of the best ways to communicate to library employees that professional learning is valued is to find ways to offer protected time for professional learning opportunities. This may involve cross-training employees so they can cover for one another as needed.

Related to the limited resource of personnel time, there is often limited or no funding available within the institution to pay for conference registration, travel, courses, and other professional development activities. If staff development is not a key initiative at the institution, funding for development opportunities will be scarce. Fortunately, there are scholarships for employees available through organizations such as the Medical Library Association (MLA) and the National Network of Libraries of Medicine (NN/LM) as well as state and regional health sciences library groups. Many of these organizations also provide development courses online at no cost. Some of the most familiar sources for free professional learning content are:

- WebJunction: This organization dubs itself "the learning place for libraries" and routinely offers free webinars for library employees on topics such as coding, STEM, data visualization, advocacy, local health data, and more.
- National Network of Libraries of Medicine: The National Library of Medicine (NN/LM-NLM) offers training for health sciences librarians across the nation through the NNLM. Live online webinars and archived content are available, training library employees to use NLM resources such as PubMed, Toxnet, MedlinePlus, and more.
- Vendor-provided webinars: Electronic resources such as Elsevier, EBSCO, Ovid, and others provide periodic training sessions on the best way to utilize common health sciences library databases.

Another resource for professional learning on limited resources involves utilizing internal opportunities within the institution. This may be available in the form of a resident expert, an internal employee with in-depth knowledge who can develop the skills of others. Additional internal opportunities may include mentors, usually associated with one-on-one development; and coaches, typically educators who are involved in project-based support.[10] Other options for internal development include organizing journal clubs, brown-bag sessions, or exchange programs for internal staff. An option for stretching development resources is a train-the-trainer model, in which one employee is sent to a developmental opportunity with the expectation that the employee will facilitate a workshop for the rest of the team.[11] Further discussion of leveraging and creating internal resources will be discussed in the training section of this chapter.

Perhaps the most challenging roadblock to professional development for library employees is an attitude that there is no need to develop new skills. While some library staff may be self-motivated to pursue development opportunities, others will consider this an added—and unwelcome—job responsibility. Health sciences libraries, like all types of libraries, have experienced continuous and rapid change for the last two decades. Regardless, some employees sincerely believe the skills they learned early in their careers will continue to meet the needs of the institution decades later.

When considering the best way to frame training/professional development sessions for library employees, a possible solution—or prevention—to this mind-set is to consider *andragogy*, or adult learning theory. Malcolm Knowles discusses six principles that drive adult learning:

1. Need to Know: Adults need to know why they are learning.
2. Self-Concept: Adults prefer to be involved in managing or even designing their learning.
3. Experience: The adult's prior experience should be taken into account and used in the learning.
4. Readiness to learn: Adults learn what is relevant to them, what they need to learn.
5. Orientation: Adults learn experientially and from problem solving.
6. Motivation: Adults are internally motivated.[12]

It's important to align staff development to the strategic goals of the library. This fits in with the "need to know" and "readiness to learn" principles. Staff will be more willing to invest time in development if they have a clear understanding about how their job and the knowledge and skills they bring to the institution make them an integral part of the team as well as an understanding about how their work ties into core initiatives within the institution.[13]

Amy Blevins, Ryan Harris, and Elizabeth Kiscaden

Nunzia B. Guise strongly encourages staff to work with their supervisors to create individually tailored plans and to ensure that work schedules are flexible enough to allow all library employees the time needed to pursue formal and informal training sessions or professional development opportunities.[14] When individuals are allowed to create their own plans and the time to pursue those plans, they are creating their own context for learning. This fits in nicely with the "self-concept" principle of adult learning. Supervisors should establish the role of learning activities within employee job descriptions, stating what percentage of time or how many developmental activities are expected within. Terminology that will be useful when building these expectations into the job description include: support for a continuous learning environment, keeping abreast of emerging trends, and a successful record of continuous development.

Recognition is a simple way to motivate to and reward employees for participation in professional development activities. Recognition may include a change in job title (if appropriate), an article in a regional newsletter, a letter from an administrator commending the employee, or the opportunity to represent the library at an event.[15] At the Annette and Irwin Eskind Biomedical Library, one incentive was a "promotion pathway." The library administrators worked with the human resources department at their institution to create a pathway based on skill acquisition. By creating a personalized learning plan, completing modules, and demonstrating the ability to apply that knowledge to their everyday responsibilities, support staff were give changes in title, pay raises, and increased responsibilities within the library.[16]

Tales from the Trenches

While writing this chapter, we wanted to get additional real-life advice from people who supervise support staff. The following are excerpts from two brief interviews conducted in September 2016.

Shelly McDavid is the access services and learning commons librarian at the Curtis Laws Wilson Library at the Missouri University of Science and Technology. She supervises six full-time and one part-time staff members, as well as nineteen student workers. She has worked in libraries since 1996, taking on a number of roles, including student assistant, circulation clerk, and library information assistant. McDavid echoed the literature in saying that while automation has definitely changed the roles for interlibrary loan and circulation, it has not reduced workloads. She feels there is a great need for professional learning opportunities for everyone who works in libraries. Recently, her library has been working to create a "culture of yes!" based on her experiences with University of Missouri Health Care.

When McDavid was asked about the best approach to providing training and professional development, she said that sometimes it has to be an expectation from the administration. In addition, it is important for everyone to have a clear understanding of expectations for professional learning and how it is related to promotions and annual evaluations. Without that, people may not take advantage of training or professional development opportunities. People get busy, delete invitations, or forget to attend events. In addition, she says it is important for staff to get to know the people they work with, find out what motivates them, and talk to them about their professional goals.[17]

Mike Wilkinson is the access services manager at the Ruth Lilly Medical Library at the Indiana University School of Medicine. He supervises a staff of six full-timers and nine part-timers in circulation and interlibrary loan. He has been working in libraries for sixteen years and has worked in circulation, interlibrary loan, and document delivery. He has seen a decrease in circulation and questions at the service desk over the years, but an increase in technology questions. Turnaround times for interlibrary loan and document delivery has greatly decreased as well.

When Wilkinson was asked about the need for training and professional development, he said that it is lower than some other places because the staff have worked at his library for a long time and are familiar with the processes and policies. As demand for service at the circulation desk has decreased and patron interactions remain mostly routine, full-time staff time has freed up for more cross-training. One of our circulation staff is working with the acquisitions department, while others have had more time to assist with shelf reading, stacks maintenance, and collection weeding. Some staff have taken advantage of committee opportunities, including the marketing committee, which strives to increase student engagement by promoting library services and technologies. It is challenging to get buy-in on new procedures and technologies from senior staff.

> I try to present benefits as much as possible and break down procedures into simpler steps. Usually written instructions are best to ensure consistency and to serve as reminders available for full- and part-time staffers who work early and late shifts at the desk. I've found one-on-one training helps solidify procedures. Group meetings, I find, are fine for introductions, but hands-on experience works best for changing work habits.[18]

Training

As mentioned earlier, training is described as being more task driven. One suggestion for working with limited budgets is to leverage internal resources and expertise. This section is devoted to several different training options.

"Tea Time Training"

The biggest resource libraries have is the people who work in the library. Therefore, one approach to take with creating in-house training sessions is to have the employees drive the training. The first step is to devote a specific time for training. In 2008, employees at East Carolina's Laupus Library for the Health Sciences were invited to participate in "Tea Time Training," which was held the first Tuesday of every month at 3:00 p.m.[19] Different people would bring in refreshments, and someone would volunteer to present a topic. One of the support staff in interlibrary loan presented a session on Twitter when it was first gaining popularity; one of the liaison librarians presented a session on resources for supporting evidence-based medicine; and so on. These events provided staff with an opportunity to learn new information, but it also offered people the chance to highlight their knowledge or skills. For those who were new to presenting or teaching, it was a safe environment in which to practice those skills.

A similar concept was used when the administration at Laupus Library decided to move to a single point-of-service model. Prior to this, the desk was always staffed by one librarian and one member of the circulation team. The librarian sat on the right side of the desk and answered reference and searching questions, while the circulation staff member sat on the left side and handled book checkouts, fines, and other traditional circulation functions. Rather than having the administrators train librarians and support staff, a team was put together that included both a librarian and a member of circulation. These two people talked to the people in their areas to learn about frustrations with both the old way of doing things and the new way of doing things. Then the training team worked together to design handouts and training sessions for the rest of the library. While the change was difficult for some people, the team that included staff from each side of the desk teaching their peers was fairly well received.

Of course, Laupus Library is not the only library to implement these types of programs. The Moody Medical Library at the University of Texas Medical Branch published an article in 1981 that detailed their staff professional development program along with the ways in which they evaluated the programs.[20] Rather than relying on a specific need (as in the single point-of-service desk) or on the presenters, the library put together a survey to identify perceived training needs. Participation, both as an instructor and as a participant, was voluntary. The only requirements were an evaluation form at the end and some sort of activity or postinstructional quiz included with the learning event. At the end of the series of instructional sessions, the library also provided its staff with the opportunity to anonymously review the programming. The sessions offered at this library were so popular that staff members were limited to two courses per person to minimize the effect on day-to-day responsibilities.

Online Modules

One of the greatest challenges to training and professional development is time. It may be difficult for support staff who work at service desks to find time to leave the office during busy periods. In addition, some support staff may feel guilty about taking time away from their busy jobs to travel, even just to another building at the institution. There may also be library employees who, for a variety of reasons, simply do not enjoy attending in-person workshops. One potential solution is to create online modules for in-house training. An example of this is a set of training modules that were created in a course management system at the University of Iowa.[21] The initial set of modules was designed to train graduate students who worked at the service desk. These modules included instruction related to: policies and procedures, database searching, evidence-based practice, finding full text, and much more. Quizzes were included for all the modules, and real-time grading allowed the students to see how well they had mastered the information. In addition, some assignments were graded by library employees. Over time, the modules were used as part of the onboarding process for new librarians as well as graduate library students.

Institution Workshops

Of course, there are situations where the expertise needed for a specific training session does not exist within the library. There may also be situations where a library employee would not be comfortable receiving training from a coworker, supervisor, or direct report. In those instances, it may be helpful to take advantage of workshops offered through different departments in the institution. Many human resources departments offer sessions for supervisors and others to learn how to navigate difficult conversations and provide meaningful feedback. Information technology departments may offer training sessions on software programs. Equal opportunity and diversity departments may offer sessions on cultural awareness. Furthermore, it may be possible to contact another department to provide a training session specifically for library employees.

Onboarding

As new people are hired, it is important to have a process for onboarding. Many institutions provide checklists to ensure that all information is communicated to a new hire. Ideally, a library will already have a system of training and professional development sessions in place that new hires can attend on their own schedules. In addition, if a library has already developed online modules for different tasks or processes, it may be best to have new employees complete modules on their own and then meet with different librarians and support staff

Amy Blevins, Ryan Harris, and Elizabeth Kiscaden

to review any areas of confusion and to discuss why certain processes are done the way they are.

When librarians and support staff are engaged in the training of new hires, the new employee gets the opportunity to meet with a wide variety of people, and the existing employees get the chance to brush up on information they may not use on a day-to-day basis. In addition, the person being trained may have fresh ideas for improving existing processes.

As previously mentioned, the University of Iowa created online modules to train its graduate reference assistants.[22] These modules were built into the on-boarding process for new librarians hired at the institution who reviewed them and then met with current librarians or support staff members to review the information in further detail.

Professional Development

While support staff receive many training opportunities within the institutions in which they work, it is also important to look at what kind of opportunities are available outside the institution. This is essential, as it can allow support staff to interact with others in the profession and also increase their own individual knowledge. In this section we will discuss some of the opportunities and challenges that support staff face in furthering their professional development.

While the definition for professional development from *Economic Times* does not explicitly state membership in professional organizations, that the definition includes learning from conferences may be taken to imply that membership in such organizations is important.[23] While this definition does not explicitly state membership in professional organizations, that the definition includes learning from conferences may be taken to imply that membership in such organizations is important. Memberships often include lower rates for attendance at conferences that provide opportunities to network with other support staff and librarians outside an individual's institution. These networking opportunities are a great way for people to discuss shared problems and solutions for library issues.

Both the Medical Library Association and the American Library Association (ALA) offer memberships to support staff. In both instances, these memberships are at a reduced rate compared to membership dues for librarians.[24] This incentive to join at a lower cost is important, as salary for support staff is typically lower than that of librarians. In 2015, the total membership of the ALA was 54,166.[25] The number of self-identified members who joined at the support staff level was only 1,814.[26] This is quite a large difference that does not reflect the many support staff members in libraries. This difference can also be seen in

MLA membership rates, where total membership in 2015 was 2,789, but there were only 35 affiliate members.[27] It may be that support staff are unaware of these reduced rates or cannot afford membership even at the lower rate. In some cases, library administrators may need to find new ways to encourage the support staff to become members in professional associations.

Library associations also have special interest groups or roundtables specifically for library support staff. For example, the Support Staff Interests Round Table is an official part of the ALA. Its mission is to address "a wide issues of concern to library staff, including but not limited to basic training programs, education, career development, job duties, and responsibilities and other related issues for the purpose of fostering communication and networking among all levels of library personnel."[28] The group also provides programming specific to issues and concerns relevant to support staff at the ALA annual meeting.

Participation in professional associations may also be encouraged through awards that specifically single out and celebrate the accomplishments of library support staff. Several chapters of the MLA provide an annual award for support staff. For example, the Medical Library Group of Southern California and Arizona has established a Paraprofessional of the Year Award to "honor an outstanding library paraprofessional in a health sciences library and recognize the critical role and important contributions library paraprofessionals make to the development and evolution of modern health sciences libraries and librarianship."[29] *Library Journal* sponsors a Paralibrarian of the Year Award, which recognizes "the essential role of paralibrarians, now the largest constituency of library workers, in providing excellent library service."[30] In both instances, a cash prize is given to award winners, who are recognized at the organization's annual meeting. This recognition, in front of an audience that is likely to be primarily librarians, is an important one and shows supports staff the value they bring to their libraries. This is a further incentive to take part in professional development opportunities.

Another opportunity that allows for professional development of library support staff is through certification programs, although not every state offers a certification program for library support staff and those that do use varying curricula. The intended audience for these certification programs also varies, as some are specifically designed for public libraries or law libraries.[31] In all cases, however, these programs require participation in a variety of educational sessions. The success of these programs has been furthered by the advent of online education programs: "As library paraprofessional education becomes more readily available by online delivery and affordable tuition, certification of library paraprofessionals becomes possible and desirable. The standardization

Amy Blevins, Ryan Harris, and Elizabeth Kiscaden

of library support staff education and certification will advance the profession-alization of a significant group of library workers."[32]

While it may be easier for staff to participate in certification programs online, there usually is a cost associated with them. This financial cost might be a burden for some library support staff. There is also a time commitment required to complete the classes for certification programs, which may be another barrier to participation.

While many states offer individual certification programs, the ALA has also created a centralized certification program: the Library Support Staff Certification (LSSC) program, which allows support staff to demonstrate their competencies and become Certified Library Support Staff. The LSSC program, developed by grants from the Institute of Museum and Library Services, began in January of 2010.[33] To complete the certification, support staff must meet eligibility requirements, including completing at least high school and working in a library for a minimum of one year over the previous five years,[34] and must also complete six of ten competency sets. These competencies include three required areas: foundations of library service, communication and teamwork, and technology. The other three competencies come from elective coursework. Certification can be completed by taking courses that are approved by the program or by developing an individual portfolio that demonstrates the candidate has a strong grasp of the knowledge in these areas.[35] All support staff who want to complete this program also must submit a one-time fee of $350, a cost that could be seen as a barrier to completion. Since the launch in 2010, approximately 135 support staff have completed the LSSC program.[36]

Additional venues for professional development for library support staff could include mentoring from their supervisors at work; participation in educational sessions with peers, including webinars and in-person trainings; and participating in leadership programs provided by their institutions. A good example of this type of leadership program is the Emerging Leaders program at the University of Maryland, Baltimore. This program is offered to all staff on the university's campus, including library employees. This program is "a professional development initiative geared towards examining universal principles of leadership with application to the culture of UMB."[37] The program takes more than a year to complete and includes a variety of seminars. Topics covered include Intercultural Development Index, Type and Leadership, Individual Accountability, and Leadership in Professional Organizations.[38] This is just one example of potential professional development opportunities that might be provided by the parent institution of a library.

Conclusion

Many of the challenges involved with encouraging and providing professional development and training can be addressed by investing time or money in the development of library employees and influencing employees to see the need—whether that motivation is personal or professional—to pursue development opportunities. As discussed earlier, thinking about adult learning theory (andragogy) can help provide a framework for ensuring that opportunities for professional development are seen as useful. In addition, recognizing people for taking the time to improve their skills and knowledge is an important part of building a culture of lifelong learning. It is essential for supervisors and other librarians to encourage support staff to participate in programs such as this and provide a flexible schedule that allows for participation while still ensuring that work is covered. A strong culture of professional development, along with a shared organizational culture, can work together to instill professional learning values.

Notes

1. Jo Webb, "Development Routes for Academic Library Support Staff," in *Developing Academic Library Staff for Future Success*, ed. Margaret Oldroyd, 97 (London: Facet Publishing, 2004).
2. Carol S. Scherrer, "Reference Librarians' Perceptions of the Issues They Face as Academic Health Information Professionals," *JMLA: Journal of the Medical Library Association* 92, no. 2 (2004), 226-32.
3. Beverly Murphy et al., "Revolution at the Library Service Desk," *Medical Reference Services Quarterly* 27, no. 4 (winter 2008): 379-93.
4. Association of Academic Health Sciences Libraries, *Annual Statistics of Medical School Libraries in the United States and Canada* (Seattle: Association of Academic Health Sciences Libraries, 2008-2015).
5. Sarah Glasser and Michael A. Arthur, "When Jobs Disappear: The Staffing Implications of the Elimination of Print Serials Management Tasks," *Serials Librarian* 60, no. 1-4 (2011): 109-13.
6. M. Kent Mayfield, "Beyond the Classroom: Self-Direction in Professional Learning," *Bulletin of the Medical Library Association* 81, no. 4 (October 1993): 426.
7. Scherrer, "Reference Librarians' Perceptions of the Issues They Face as Academic Health Information Professionals," 2; Nunzia B. Guise et al., "Developing a Culture of Lifelong Learning in a Library Environment," *Bulletin of the Medical Library Association* 87, no. 1 (January 1999): 26-36.
8. "Definition of 'Professional Development,'" *Economic Times*, accessed September 30, 2016, http://economictimes.indiatimes.com/definition/professional-development.
9. "Training," Merriam-Webster.com, accessed September 30, 2016, http://www.merriam-webster.com/dictionary/training.
10. Andrea W. Stewart et al. *Staff Development: A Practical Guide*, 4th ed. (Chicago: American Library Association, 2013), 6-7.

11. Anne Grodzins Lipow et al. *Staff Development: A Practical Guide* (Chicago: American Library Association, 1992), 60–61.

12. Malcolm Knowles, *The Modern Practice of Adult Education: From Pedagogy to Andragogy*, rev. ed. (Chicago: Association Press/Follet Publishing, 1980), 41–57.

13. Stewart et al., *Staff Development*, 10.

14. Guise, "Developing a Culture of Lifelong Learning in a Library Environment," 7.

15. Marcia Trotta, *Successful Staff Development: A How-to-Do-It Manual* (New York: Neal-Schuman Publishers, 1995), 99–103.

16. Ibid., 99–103.

17. Shelly McDavid, personal communication with Amy Blevins, September 22, 2016.

18. Ibid.

19. Michael Wilkinson, personal communication with Amy Blevins, September 20, 2016.

20. Elizabeth K. Eaton, "Library Staff Development Course," *Bulletin of the Medical Library Association* 69, no. 3 (July 1981): 317–21.

21. Kathryn J. Skhal and Catherine Thureson, "Iconic Training: Use of a Course Management System to Provide Continual Reference Student Education," *Medical Reference Services Quarterly* 26, no. 2 (summer 2007): 15–25.

22. Ibid.

23. "Definition of 'Professional Development,'" 8. Accessed September 30, 2016.

24. American Library Association, "ALA Personal Membership," accessed September 30, 2016, http://www.ala.org/membership/ala-personal-membership; Medical Library Association, "MLA: About: Membership Categories & Benefits," accessed September 30, 2016. http://www.mlanet.org/p/cm/ld/fid=447.

25. American Library Association, "ALA Annual Membership Statistics," accessed September 30, 2016, http://www.ala.org/membership/membershipstats_files/annual _memb_stats.

26. Ron Jankowski, e-mail to Ryan Harris, September 12, 2016.

27. Kate Corcoran, e-mail to Ryan Harris, September 14, 2016.

28. American Library Association, "Library Support Staff Interests Round Table (LS-SIRT)," accessed September 30, 2016, http://www.ala.org/lssirt.

29. Medical Library Group of Southern California Arizona, "Paraprofessional of the Year Award," accessed September 30, 2016, http://mlgsca.mlanet.org/beta/index.php/ awards/paraprofessional-of-the-year-award.

30. Library Journal, "Paralibrarian of the Year Nomination Guidelines," accessed September 30, 2016, http://lj.libraryjournal.com/awards/paralibrarian-of-the-year-nomi nation-guidelines/#_ .

31. American Library Association, "Library Support Staff Certification Information by State," accessed September 30, 2016, http://www.ala.org/offices/library-sup port-staff-certification-information-state.

32. Martha J. Birchfield, "Certificate and Associate Degree Education for Library Paraprofessionals: Distance Makes It Possible," *Journal of Access Services* 2, no. 3 (2004): 44.

33. American Library Association, "About LSSC," Library Support Staff Certification website, accessed September 30, 2016, http://ala-apa.org/lssc/about-lssc.

34. American Library Association, "Candidate Application, Eligibility, and Cost," Library Support Staff Certification website, accessed September 30, 2016, http://ala-apa .org/lssc/for-candidates/eligibility-and-cost.

35. American Library Association, "Competency Sets," Library Support Staff Certification website, accessed September 30, 2016, http://ala-apa.org/lssc/for-candidates/competency-sets.
36. Kimberly Redd, e-mail to Ryan Harris, September 13, 2016.
37. University of Maryland Baltimore, "Emerging Leaders," accessed September 30, 2016, http://www.umaryland.edu/hrs/current-employees/organization-and-employee-development/umb-employee-development-and-learning/emerging-leaders.
38. University of Maryland Baltimore, "Curriculum—Emerging Leaders," accessed September 30, 2016, http://www.umaryland.edu/hrs/current-employees/organization-and-employee-development/umb-employee-development-and-learning/emerging-leaders/curriculum.

Chapter 4

Creating the Nimble Organization

Jean P. Shipman and Mary Joan (M. J.) Tooey

Definition of a Nimble Organization

To discuss the creation and nurturing of a nimble organization, a definition of a *nimble organization* is needed. One advertising firm defines "organizational nimbleness as the ability and willingness to make smart and timely decisions about core organizational strategies, resources and actions based on real-world dynamics."[1] This means an organization needs to be a part of, and be rapidly responsive to, economic, political, technological, cultural, and global forces. The organization needs to be proactive, capturing opportunities as they surface rather than waiting until it is too late to make effective and advantageous decisions. While a late decision may be a great one, if the timing is too late, the decision is worthless.

Benefits of a Nimble Organization

The benefits to being a nimble organization are alluded to in the definition above, specifically, the ability to be proactive and opportunistic. Within any large organization, there are always those groups that seem to be leading the way and on the cutting edge of trends and strategic directions. These are units that always seem to be innovative and ready with ideas, functioning well as teams and adddding value to whatever they undertake. They are sought-after partners because they elevate projects. Returning to the definition of a nimble organization, these groups and their members have found methods for gathering information on multiple aspects of an organization and determining how to apply and act on that information with agility and nimbleness. They seem to be effective and swift decision makers. They are not afraid to make mistakes, learn from them, and correct them quickly. They are resilient. They have discovered that being nimble is a strategic advantage.

Nimbleness focuses on empowering the individual. Organizations are composed of individuals, so it is incumbent upon leadership to nurture nimbleness up, down, and across the organizational chart. This encourages all members of the organizational team to seek opportunities and to act independently in swift response to these opportunities. To enable this, leadership must clearly articulate organizational goals, objectives, and strategies so that everyone understands them and there is no question regarding the appropriateness of acting on opportunities. Effective communication channels are needed to encourage open information sharing regarding opportunities, approaches, appropriate responses, and solutions.

Characteristics of Nimble Organizations

An overview of the literature around nimble organizations reveals characteristics such as quick response to strategic opportunities, shorter decision cycles, a focus on change, integration of the customer voice and user experience, and the building of interdisciplinary project teams. Although these characteristics are primarily in the business literature, they can easily be applied to libraries. The ability to act quickly when presented with opportunities or challenges is critical. Swift decision making can often be the difference between a lost opportunity and a transformative one. Constant knowledge of the user fueled by assessment enables informed decision making. A critical knowledge base enables ease of decision making. Building empowered and diverse teams creates trust. Nimbleness is an intentional management strategy.

How Is Nimbleness Achieved?

Within every library there are opportunities to apply the characteristics of nimble organizations. These opportunities differ from library to library. Some libraries focus on strategic opportunities, others on interdisciplinary teams and partnerships. Understanding institutional priorities, and aligning library goals with them, is an initial step to becoming a nimble organization.

Pillars of Effort

One method for strategically mapping a path to become a nimble organization is to identify and outline the main pillars that exist within a library's infrastructure and work ethos, and then funnel and filter new opportunities though these

Jean P. Shipman and Mary Joan (M. J.) Tooey

pillars. For example, the strategic plan for 2016-2018 at the Spencer S. Eccles Health Sciences Library at the University of Utah, includes three pillars. Initiatives are prioritized and categorized through the three pillars of *evidence, scholarly engagement,* and *educational technology.* These three pillars are supported by a foundation of partnership and collaboration. Three key goals matching the University of Utah goals include:

- promoting and improving patient care, health, and quality of life;
- enabling and enhancing learner success; and
- fostering and engaging in discovery and innovation.

Achievement of these goals will be shaped through consideration of the three strategic pillars and their foundation.

Strategic Alignment

Another approach to the development of a nimble organization was taken at the Health Sciences and Human Services Library (HS/HSL) at the University of Maryland, Baltimore (UMB). Through an intensive user-focused strategic planning process aligned with university priorities, the library team engaged the UMB community in a conversation defining library partnerships for the success of its users. Within the HS/HSL's foci of *expertise, resources,* and *place,* the six library strategic themes are in alignment with UMB's strategic themes of *health, justice and social impact; research and scholarship; student success; inclusive excellence; partnership and collaboration;* and *efficiency, effectiveness, and assessment.*

These themes provide a framework for almost every aspect of the HS/HSL team's work and projects. Understanding and internalization of these themes enables agile and quick response to university priorities and environmental changes, encouraging interdisciplinary and interprofessional partnerships and a team approach to problem solving, and, finally, translating into individual performance plans and objectives. This individual understanding and alignment with UMB's priorities enables independent, empowered, and swift approaches to decision making.

Enabling Nimbleness

There are a number of attributes that enable and support a nimble organization.

Organizational Size

Health sciences libraries tend to be smaller than academic or public libraries, and thus have the flexibility to handle changes to established strategy, consider new proposals and opportunities, and reach consensus more easily.

Smaller organizations can be more nimble and agile, as communication with fewer people is often easier. Strategic directions can be discussed informally with a smaller number of individuals.

Buy-In and Decision Making

Many organizations strive for consensus when reaching decisions, but by definition, consensus does not mean everyone agrees with decisions that are reached. Consensus means that individuals are aware of the issues and the considerations needed to reach decisions, and that individuals agree to carry out final decisions even if they are not in favor of them. Consensus can thus lead to greater staff buy-in regarding decisions because consensus can frequently be arrived at more quickly than total agreement.

Speed in decision making is an important feature of nimble organizations. Individuals need to understand and accept that certain decisions may need to be made rapidly and unilaterally, without reaching consensus, to avoid missed opportunities or to ensure safety or mitigate harm. This kind of rapid decision making may happen in the case of an opportunity that must be immediately acted upon or it will be lost. These opportunities may involve financial support, such as gifts, or opportunities for partnerships or collaborations. Decisions may have to be made quickly to prevent harm or extensive damage to people, equipment, facilities, or collections. Personal safety also may necessitate quick decisions. In these cases, there must be an implicit agreement that an individual may need to make a decision without consulting others.

Facility Design

Nimble organizations create environments, public and private, that encourage creative processes and brainstorming. Publicly designed spaces encourage groups or partners to work closely together with the tools they need to be effective and efficient. Spaces such as the Innovation Space at the UMB's HS/HSL are developed to provide a place for experimentation and creativity. Due to the rigidity of curricula and the continuing silos at UMB, opportunities did not exist for students and faculty to come together to investigate new technologies or processes. Therefore, an opportunity existed where the library could play an important role. A team at the library was swiftly formed to develop a white paper and plan for developing an innovation space within the library.[2] There was already a model for this swift response with the library's Presentation Practice Studio, which had been developed in response to student requests. With funding provided by a generous donor, the Innovation Space was opened on the main floor of the library in April 2015, and was doubled in size by November 2016. Containing 3-D printers and scanners, a button maker, specialized technology training software, a DNA model, Google Cardboard, and other interest-

Jean P. Shipman and Mary Joan (M. J.) Tooey

ing gadgets, the Innovation Space has become the locus of creative activity not only for students, but for faculty, as well as clinical staff. This has led to library partnerships with the university's Institute for Genomic Sciences, the Shock Trauma Center, and several departments requiring modeling capabilities.[3] A monthly newsletter reports on use of the space, special events take place in the space, and classes have been developed and offered on emerging technologies and software there. Future plans include adding high-end graphics, editing capabilities, and virtual reality, along with a consideration of additional innovation space.

At the EHSL, an Ideation Studio[4] was created to offer groups and teams a place to gather to solicit and share ideas, discuss possible paths to take, and reach potential resolutions to problems, as well as to shape desired outcomes and achieve goals. Group efforts are facilitated through the provision of tools and widgets housed in movable carts. Widgets include pipe cleaners, nuts and bolts, springs, stress balls, popsicle sticks, and other items, as well as an assortment of household tools such as screwdrivers, wrenches, and tweezers. This Ideation Studio is located on the main library floor and is somewhat defined by movable telescopic white walls that offer flexibility in the size of group spaces and provide some privacy. The Ideation Studio is located near equipment, including video and audio program creation stations, as well as librarians who can offer assistance and guidance to the groups based on their needs. Similar spaces[5] have been created at other institutions, such as the Kiva Group Think at Virginia Tech.[6]

No less important are the staff spaces supportive of nimbleness. Whether staff are colocated within a library or distributed into user environments, effective work and collaborative spaces are essential for encouraging nimble behavior and creativity. Things as simple as light and open workspaces can make it enjoyable to come to work. Staff access to technology—ranging from new technologies to personal laptops and multiple screens at workstations—can increase productivity and job satisfaction. Collaborative workrooms and places to meet and gather also positively impact job satisfaction. Abraham Maslow's hierarchy tells us that if basic human needs, such as shelter and safety, are met, we are enabled to move onto higher areas of growth, development, and self-actualization.[7] Becoming nimble and thinking and acting with agility fall into those higher areas.

Enabling Nimbleness

The desire to be a nimble organization is frequently identified by library leadership; however, becoming a nimble organization requires buy-in from and participation of all library team members. The cultivation and development of a nimble culture begins with the hiring process and continues throughout the work life span. Staff often account for more than 50 percent of a library's budget and are the greatest asset when it comes to creativity and nimbleness.

Hiring

The first trick to creating nimble organizations is hiring the right kind of person to work in such an environment. An important characteristic of this kind of staff member is a willingness to explore new ideas and then pivot on these ideas if new directions come along or if new approaches are needed. These individuals seek and thrive on change, discovering new methods for any kind of process and continually striving for improvement. How does one hire someone with such characteristics? It is important to state in the job announcement that the ideal candidate is someone who enjoys change and is willing to work within a nimble environment. During the interview process, ask questions requiring candidates to describe work situations in which they exhibited a high degree of flexibility or guided a group through a major change in direction, and find out how they were able to do this. Share with candidates the types of changes your library has executed and see how they react to these situations. Ask their opinions about how they would have approached the challenges; it is fairly easy to tell who is comfortable with change and who is not.

Training

Can nimbleness be taught? A quick Google search results in numerous offerings, from agility skill development to nimble sales training classes to innovative processes. There are many courses and sessions that showcase nimble organizational examples and characteristics. Personal attribute training is also available. It may be helpful to bring in a speaker, allowing staff to hear the same message in order to develop and reinforce an organizational culture that seeks and rewards nimble behaviors. There are also webinars that demonstrate nimble attributes and skills. A great way to transfer knowledge from other domains is to attend a professional conference outside of librarianship that has a focus on nimble behavior in order to learn how that profession values and trains for nimbleness. Often, reading another domain's professional literature provides insights into how others respect and cultivate agile behavior phenotypes. Stepping outside one's own box and exploring how other domains treat similar issues and topics can be one of the most liberating training techniques available. It forces one to take a different perspective on common problems and issues, often resulting in fresh solutions and approaches. Look for synergies with other professions that can transform into beneficial partnerships or collaborations.

Cross-Training

Cross-training involves training individuals within an organization to cover for different units; an additional outcome of cross-training is that it gives staff an increased awareness of one another's roles, values, and challenges.

Cross-training can be a means of ensuring that all vital aspects of an organization can operate at all times, but it can also be a terrific way to allow fresh eyes to address chronic problems, suggesting new solutions and outcomes. Individuals can be encouraged, while being cross-trained, to use several lean tools, such as the 5 Whys or the Swim Lane, to help to understand which process steps are crucial and which are remnants of past needs, sacred cows, or outdated operating modes.[8]

Rewards and Incentives

As an organization moves toward becoming more nimble, it should consider early on how to reward nimble behaviors, innovative thinkers and doers, and risk takers. If an organization is truly pushing its envelope, failures should occur frequently. Failure, as well as success, needs to be rewarded and encouraged. Individuals should work within safe and supportive environments where achievers can take on a different persona: for example, generating new program interests or trying—and failing—a new program. In these cases, individuals have gone beyond the norm and attempted new approaches and creative problem solving, which is much of what being nimble is all about. The Japanese proverb "Fall down seven times and get up eight" means that the only true failure is quitting.[9] Resilience is critical for a nimble organization, and both success and failure should be rewarded. Additionally, support for flexible hours, professional participation and development, and recognition for work well done are essential for growing a nimble culture. Meaningful meetings and programs in which all viewpoints are encouraged and acknowledged reinforces the value of the nimble individual, while also reinforcing nimbleness in support of joint library and institutional goals.

Empowerment and Trust

Empowerment and trust are at the core of any nimble organization. It is to the advantage of every organization aspiring to be nimble to embrace these concepts, which frequently go hand in hand. Trust is actually bidirectional. Team members must trust in the leadership of the team to establish foundational truths regarding the work to be done. Leaders must trust in team members and believe they are in sync with organizational goals and cultures. This involves open and honest communication regarding all aspects and nuances of projects, politics, and potential opportunities.

Without this bidirectional trust, it is difficult to encourage independent decision making and direction setting. It is difficult to empower team members to be nimble and agile in seizing opportunities. An additional benefit to building this trust, which is supportive of the development of a nimble organization, is that leadership development occurs organically: individuals or nonhierarchical teams are given permission to find and seize opportunities and make decisions when they arise without waiting for administrative direction. One caution, though, is that communication channels must be active and open so that everyone knows what is going on, and who is doing what, in order to mitigate confusion or error.

Funding

Creating Alternative Funding Streams

Library funding often comes from many sources, depending on the private or public nature of the parent institution. When nimbleness is restricted by the lack of money to tackle a new project or implement a new program, it may be critical to seek extramural funding, following institutional fund-raising guidelines. These funds can come from donors, governmental grants or contracts, foundations, or internal institutional seed grants. Sometimes institutions offer pilot study funding to test new concepts or ideas. Revenue-generating programs can also be a source of new funding. The incorporation of costs into associated service fees, where applicable, offers an opportunity to provide a service that would otherwise not be affordable.

Relationships and Funding

Relationships resulting from funding need to be nurtured just as much as those created. When funding is involved, the work group is often dictated by the funding source. This partnership may exist only as long as the funding period, but these working relationships can also turn into longer partnerships that outlast the funding cycle. Whatever the length of the partnership, one of the key requirements of receiving funding is for the library to be a good steward of the funding and to ensure that communication with the funders is transparent and frequent. Funders want their support to make a difference. Being willing to engage funders and team members in the process is one way to build relationships. If funders are not part of the processes, they should be kept in the loop about progress, challenges, results, and outcomes, so they feel their contribution is appreciated and has made a difference. They should be introduced to key team members so they have faces to attach to names. The internal benefit of this is that members of the team feel included and empowered and have the opportunity to learn what is important to funders. Demonstrating the impact of the funding, both within the institution and publicly, helps to keep funders in the loop. Inviting funders to participate in celebratory events, including them in publicity materials, considering them part of the extended team, and touching base with them often, are other ways to ensure they feel included and appreciated.

Jean P. Shipman and Mary Joan (M. J.) Tooey

Effective Partnerships and Collaborations

In today's rapidly changing world, partnerships and collaborations can be the most productive and valuable solutions available to libraries to survive and flourish. Partnerships and collaborations are seedbeds for nimble organizations, providing opportunities to try new and exciting things. Partnerships and collaborations can be of many varieties: among libraries, between units within a university, between individuals, among groups, and among institutions. Is there a difference between the words *partnership* and *collaboration*? Partnerships are activities occurring between two individuals, groups, or units, such as a marriage or a sale. From a legal standpoint, partnerships may involve an explicit or implicit contractual obligation and can be construed as being more formal, with each entity accepting risks and benefits. Collaborations, on the other hand, usually involve two or more individuals, groups, or units and are limitless in size and are oriented toward relationships or people.[10] There are many articles and books that deal with the topic of building successful partnerships and collaborations, so this chapter will not address these aspects, instead focusing on the benefits to health sciences libraries.

Working in partnership and collaboration can be something asked of you and your library or something you initiate. Combination of individuals or units to work together is more advantageous than going it alone. The combined efforts may have more impact because of the number of people involved, who is involved, potential and beneficial group achievements, changes initiated, or novel approaches taken. Collective efforts should be more productive and beneficial than solo ones.

Components of an Effective Partnership or Collaboration

The best and most nimble partnerships and collaborations are built on trust and mutual respect. Each party enters into these arrangements with the belief that working together will confer some sort of benefit to all those involved. Resources may be pooled, talent may be rounded, communities may be combined in new and unique ways, and those targeted will appreciate and benefit from the efforts of all involved.

Partnerships and collaborations usually start as conversations around a shared problem, mutual needs, or opportunities resulting from special funding or community support. They also can result from a formal charge from university leaders, from community officials, or from individuals, all of whom share a vision as to how combined efforts will lead to a greater good. If no formal charge is issued, parties involved in partnerships or collaborations should create a charter or documented structure for how they imagine working together, who will receive credit and how credit will be given, and what resources will be contributed by each party. Once these basic premises are agreed upon, strategic directions with stated goals, objectives, and actionable items should be outlined and shared with all members. A time line should also be formulated, as should success measures, including metrics to be gathered and assessed along the way. Outcomes of the combined efforts should also be agreed upon, and action plans should be developed to ensure the achievement of desired outcomes. These agreements are usually not contractual in basis, but more along the lines of memorandums of agreement or understanding, although contracts may come into play depending upon the units involved and the institutional policies that must be followed.

Starting New Partnerships or Collaborations

If you or your library could benefit by being more visible and active in your institution, consider volunteering to lead or be a team member of a university-wide committee or initiative. This offers a chance to professionally develop leadership skills and enhance group dynamic management talents. It also gives the library a place at the table and identifies potential involvement in activities that others would not have even considered. Being vocal and informative about the breadth of what librarians and staff can offer often leads to new partnering or collaborative opportunities. It is also an opportunity to "voluntell" members of your team to participate in different committees or initiatives. Delegation is a powerful trust builder within organizations, and the same benefits related to leadership skills and group dynamic work can be accrued by library team members.

Obstacles to Nimbleness

Are there obstacles to being a nimble library? Of course there are. Within this chapter, the cornerstones of trust and empowerment have been discussed as essential. Developing a nimble organization is hard work. It requires clarity of vision and a continuous commitment to, and modeling of, those cornerstones, not only by library leadership but also by those entrusted and empowered with being nimble. Creating a nimble organization inherently creates a pact among all involved.

Obstacles can be of three types: *organizational, attitudinal,* or *behavioral.*[11] Organizationally, an institution may not support nimble principles or behaviors. Organizational leadership may not trust that the library team can take on a task, or even that the task is appropriate for the library. There can be attitudinal issues by library leadership who may *talk the talk* rather than *walk the walk* regarding their commitment to developing a nimble organization. Behavioral issues such as passive-aggressiveness regarding taking on responsibilities or challenges can often get in the way. Old habits die hard, and many team members may fear

Jean P. Shipman and Mary Joan (M. J.) Tooey

reprisal for making mistakes. They may need to overanalyze situations in order to mitigate risks. They may feel more comfortable referring decision making upward. These are barriers to overcome. The creation of a nimble organization often involves a cultural change.

The Future

Change is nothing new, and many say it is the only constant in life. Nimbleness is one way of dealing with change. The speed of change will continue to accelerate as new innovations are encouraged and generated, and new solutions for past problems are instituted. In their book *Tension: The Energy of Innovation*,[12] Chris and Mitch Wasden outline three strategies. They state the role for leaders to create innovative and nimble environments that permit employees to be creative and productive. Leaders need to ensure that their workforce is equipped with the skills, attributes, and comfort to deal with rapid change and uncertainty. Failure to create safe and talented work environments will create gaps in strategic understanding, productivity, and employee satisfaction. Employees are the library's most treasured resource; a leader's strong vision of how to effectively manage and create change that adapts to employee situations will enable the library to succeed in the future.

Conclusion

Can an organization be too nimble? Are there consequences for being too nimble or not nimble enough? Are there guidelines and metrics available to measure nimbleness? Unfortunately, nimbleness is a soft concept, and hard metrics do not yet exist to measure it. As external forces apply more pressure to organizations, the ability to adjust rapidly and flourish within chaos is becoming an important attribute for organizations to possess. Often, those working in libraries ask, "Can we just slow down a minute and not accept the new opportunities that are offered by our users, our university units, or externally? Can we be okay for the moment and not feel the need to continually monitor our progress and our situations?" With more pressure for accountability on publicly funded institutions, the answer is "probably not." As technology advances at an exponential rate and as economic factors require all aspects of the enterprise to do more with less, the constant quest for more efficient and effective processes is here to stay. The need to thrive in these shifting environments is the reason nimbleness is highly desired. The environment in which we work today requires us to focus and function amidst shifting parameters and mandates. No one has the ultimate answer as to how to stop or slow down change; we can only react to it and to learn how to proactively approach it. These skills are what enable some libraries to thrive and survive, while others fold. While nimbleness is a soft concept, it is hard to achieve without the willingness of employees. Creating a culture of nimbleness is a key way to shape the future and to ensure that libraries remain vibrant and relevant to educators, researchers, health-care professionals, and students.

We hope this chapter has encouraged you to adopt ways of becoming more nimble in your thinking, your strategy, and your achievements, and to increase your *nimbility*, both personally and professionally. To paraphrase a famous nursery rhyme: be nimble, be quick, and be ready to jump those candlesticks that you face as you develop your nimble organization.

Notes

1. Ascent Advising, "Nimble; The New Big," accessed June 4, 2016, http://www.ascent advising.com/?p=321.
2. Bohyun Kim et al., "Makerspace Task Force Report," University of Maryland Digital Archive, 2014, accessed June 27, 2016, http://hdl.handle.net/10713/4634.
3. HS/HSL Innovation Space website. Accessed July 23, 2017. http://www.hshsl.un-maryland.edu/services/ispace.
4. Jean Shipman, "Ideation Studio Opens!" [Synapse: newsletter of the Spencer S. Eccles Health Sciences Library, 2016 July–September (vol 31 no 3), accessed July 22, 2017, (https://library.med.utah.edu/synapse/2016-july-september-vol-31/ideation-studio-opens/
5. id@vt, "Facilities," 2013, accessed July 22, 2017. https//www.industrial design.arch.vt.edu/
6. H. Rex Hartson and Pardha S. Pyla, "Design Thinking, Ideation, and Sketching," in *The UX Book: Process and Guidelines for Ensuring a Quality User Experience*, 251–97 (Amsterdam: Elsevier, 2012).
7. "Maslow's Hierarchy of Needs," Wikipedia, accessed November 4, 2016, https://en.wikipedia.org/wiki/Maslow's_hierarchy_of_needs.
8. James P. Womack, Daniel T. Jones, and Daniel Roos, *The Machine That Changed the World: The Story of Lean Production* (New York: Free Press, 1990).
9. "Japanese Proverbs," Wikipedia, accessed November 4, 2016, https://en.wikipedia.org/wiki/Japanese_proverbs.
10. Greer Glazer, Charles Alexandre, and Patricia Reid Ponte. "Legislative: Partnership or Collaboration: Words Matter." *Online Journal of Issues in Nursing* 13, no. 2 (2008), accessed November 4, 2016, http://www.nursingworld.org/MainMenuCategories/ANAMarketplace/ANAPeriodicals/OJIN/TableofContents/vol132008/No-2May08/PartnershiporCollaboration.html.
11. "Building a Nimble Organization: A McKinsey Global Survey," *McKinsey Quarterly*, 2006. accessed November 4, 2016, http://leadway.org/PDF/Building%20A%20Nimble%20Organization.pdf.
12. Chris Wasden and Mitch Wasden, *Tension: The Energy of Innovation* (Midway, UT: Scipio Press, 2015), 237–38.

Chapter 5

Communication

Heather N. Holmes, Shannon D. Jones, and Ana Reeves

communication |kə,myōōnə'kāSH(ə)n| noun
The act or process of using words, sounds, signs, or behaviors to express or exchange information or to express your ideas, thoughts, feelings, etc., to someone else.[1]

Remember the telephone game? Think back to elementary school. Many teachers use the game as a means to instruct young learners in the art of communication. The teacher gathers students in a circle and has them pass a message from one person to the next by whispering in the person's ear. By the time the message passes through a few students it has already changed, and by the time it reaches the end of the line it is even more convoluted. The telephone game is a perfect analogy for how communication can break down: the message received may not be what was intended.

Like all organizations, libraries rely on communication to function. The size of the organization doesn't matter; single-person and start-up companies rely on communication just as much as multimillion-dollar businesses with thousands of employees do. Without effective communication, the organization will suffer. In libraries, where the main focus is on the delivery of information, communication must be effective between individuals and between groups of people, including students, colleagues, and administrators.

At the Medical University of South Carolina's Libraries (MUSC), a change in leadership took place between 2015 and 2016. After serving about twenty-five years in the position, the Libraries' director retired and a new one was hired. Seven months later a new associate director was hired, and the library underwent some major changes, with new styles and avenues of communication explored. Both staff and leadership have learned lessons through these changes, and continue to learn each day. This chapter highlights some of what was learned in the ongoing effort to communicate effectively in an academic library setting.

What is effective communication? The definition at the beginning of the chapter states that effective communication is imparting or exchanging information. Simply exchanging information, however, doesn't mean that the communication is effective. Imparting or exchanging information is only one aspect of communication. The recipient not only needs to receive and understand the information being communicated, but also needs to take the information and put it to use. Effective communication requires at least one recipient, but in the case of libraries there are often many recipients, including colleagues, members of the larger organization, and library users.

What if the library implements a new procedure for placing interlibrary loan (ILL) requests? Since this new procedure will affect many library users, communication needs to be more clear, concise, and easy to understand than if it was intended for only one user. A sign could be hung near the library's front door alerting users to the change in procedure, but that would most likely result in a communication breakdown. Many users would never see the sign. Others may see it but not know what ILL is, even if it is a service they use regularly. When communicating something that will affect many people, potentially in many different ways, signage is only one method to deliver the message. A change in procedure for something as big as ILL will need to be communicated in many ways in order to reach as wide of an audience as possible.

It is important to communicate information to the right audience at the right time and place. Taking it a step further, it is important to make sure that the right amount of information is delivered. In today's world, information overload is very real, so ensuring that the right amount of information is delivered ensures efficient, effective communication.

Using our example of implementing a new ILL request procedure can involve many stages: from considering the change, through developing the process, to final rollout and implementation, as well as overcoming the obstacles encountered along the way. Developing an effective communication plan needs to be a consideration from the very beginning. Implementing a new ILL procedure may involve less paper and more digital transfer, changing response times and fees, an expanding clientele base, and new equipment or staff—all moving parts that need to be considered carefully.

Heather N. Holmes, Shannon D. Jones, and Ana Reeves

A communication plan ensures that the new procedural information is carefully evaluated before it is launched to users, when any defects will quickly become apparent and potentially cause a loss of trust. There may be more than one procedure evaluated, each based on what type of audience will be receiving it. New information—for whatever purpose and for whatever audience—should be presented in as concise, clear, and logical fashion as possible. Too much superfluous, ambiguous, or confusing information is not good practice.

Consider the Audience

The audience, as the user or consumer of information, plays perhaps the biggest role in deciding whether communication thrives or withers. Whether working with a new group or one that has long been established, if there are consistent problems with communication, consider a healthy "reboot" with the audience and examine ways to adjust the methods being used. Evolving technology constantly provides new methods of reaching audiences. Taking advantage of the best technology for a particular audience can be a real game changer in delivering effective communication. Examples of this will be discussed later in this chapter.

When disseminating information, one often overlooked consideration is how the audience needs or prefers the material to be delivered. At the MUSC Libraries, observation and experience informed us about how the staff best digested information. Simply asking questions is a direct way to discover the best delivery method and to gauge how well your audience understands the material. This feedback will help in designing better messages. An additional consideration is that preferences may change based on the information or topic being communicated. Using a combination of observation and direct input from the audience, one can create a plan of communication using a mix of methods and tools to meet any need.

The audience is essential to communication because even a basic message requires participation. Truly effective communication requires not only participation but reciprocation. The roles of information broadcaster and audience often alternate in an ongoing exchange. This allows both sides to see how messages are being interpreted, and determines what method of communication will be most beneficial going forward.

One suggestion to consider is asking the audience to demonstrate trust and a vested interest in their needs: How do they process information? Do they need visual or verbal communication, or both? Do they prefer digital or hard copies of flyers, notices, and so forth?

There can be many reasons why a response isn't received. Perhaps the delivery method is wrong, the message is confusing; it may have been misinterpreted. When soliciting a response, the requester should always provide a reason why he or she is requesting input. Is it to make a change? Is it for data collection? Providing a reason will make a response more likely because respondents know they are providing something of value.

Consider the Method

How do effective managers communicate with their staff? How do they receive and accept feedback? How do they demonstrate that a staff member has absorbed and understood a message? Remembering the role of an audience member helps when crafting a message.

When a manager is conducting a meeting, it should be structured with a clear agenda. Most people already feel there isn't enough time in the day to get all their work done, so it should be no surprise that many employees feel meetings are a waste of time. Sitting through meetings that are poorly organized makes the audience wonder how or why the information is relevant to them. When planning a meeting, ensure the right people are invited, and then deliver the right amount of information.

Is a meeting even necessary? Could the information be delivered via e-mail? Choosing the appropriate delivery method is just as important as the content of the message. A meeting may be called for any number of reasons, but it is important to consider whether it is necessary to draw the audience away from their daily tasks to deliver the message.

The basic foundation of communication strategy is to make sure the message addresses questions of *who, what, where, why, when,* and *how.* This may seem straightforward, but how many times has confusion ensued over using a phrase such as "next Wednesday" or "the following Wednesday" to announce a meeting, when using the actual date would make the message clear? In e-mail communication, appropriate use of the subject line can make a difference as to whether a message is even opened, let alone read. Deciding whether too much (or not enough) information is being communicated depends on the audience, so the sender needs to gain an understanding of who his or her audience is and what their needs are. Following is a more in-depth discussion of some of the communication methods explored at MUSC, along with lessons learned about using each of them.

Verbal Communication

Verbal communication is great for relaying quick messages or checking in with someone. It often implies a more casual feeling than communication by e-mail;

for example, verbally asking someone how a project is progressing avoids unintended pressure and creates more of an open dialogue. Verbal communication is also best for more complicated situations, or where there are several details that need to be discussed.

Facial and body language are also important. Some people read these behaviors better than others. For positive verbal communication, be sure to turn toward the speaker, listen actively, maintain eye contact, and respond with a verbal acknowledgment of what is being said. If appropriate for the conversation, a smile can go a long way in making someone feel more comfortable. Facial and body language are also important. Some people read these behaviors better than others so be patient, give cues, paraphrase their statements, and if appropriate, be sure to send a written follow-up afterward. Also be sure to consider tone, both while speaking and in follow-up, because the impact can be significant. Sarcasm, gruffness, or increased volume can make people nervous or angry and impede open communication.

People have different needs and preferences. If an employee is not a great auditory learner, has social anxiety, or struggles with verbal conversation, then adjust the conversation. It's not a matter of avoiding verbal communication; however, it is important to remember that there are other methods that may work better for some employees. Include or follow up with formats that give the receiver a better chance to successfully receive and respond to the message. Bring handouts to discussions, post notes, share slides, and record trainings.

Communication by Telephone

Face-to-face communication is very effective, but the telephone is often a necessary alternative. While engaged in a phone conversation, or immediately thereafter, it may be helpful to take notes. The human memory is often flawed, so a phone log can provide a useful reference to what was discussed. This can preclude critical information from slipping through the cracks, and avoid the "he said, she said" syndrome if any questions come up later. Voicemail messages, although easily erased, do leave a record for the recipient. When leaving a voicemail message, be sure to identify yourself and your reason for calling. For example, you may say "Hi Michael, this is Heather. I'm calling to follow up on the conversation we had last week about implementing a new interlibrary loan protocol. Please call me back when you're able. Thanks."

The importance of body language and tone still applies to phone conversations. If there is obvious tension, try smiling; it makes a difference to the sound of your voice. If distractions occur while you are talking, stand up and walk around. A good listener can tell when someone is distracted.

E-mail Communication

Many people have a love-hate relationship with e-mail: for all the agony of an overstuffed inbox, there will be that gem about leftover cake in the staff room. E-mail may be less popular in social circles where people use various phone apps and social media, but in the work environment it is still a standard form of communication.

E-mail can be used to quickly relay messages to a large number of people simultaneously. It is an easy way to follow up on a conversation or group discussion. It enables communication with employees who have issues with verbal communication. It is also valuable in tracking exchanges and maintaining a communication history.

Less is more when crafting an e-mail message. Bullet points can be useful when providing specific information. Subject lines are important because they provide the headline of the message. Consider adding a qualifier of FYI or NNTR (no need to respond) to the subject line in order to give the recipient a notice of the urgency of the message. If possible, never use e-mail as the sole method of communication for urgent information. These days more and more people are generally "connected" via smartphone and tend to be more accessible to get messages even if they're not at their computer; however, if an urgent message needs to be communicated it is best to use multiple methods to reach as many people as possible.

Obviously, e-mail may not be the best route for sensitive or complicated matters, where the advantages of face-to-face—or at least verbal—communication make it more appropriate. Also beware of using group e-mails to relay information that should be presented in a meeting; this can become a protracted and sporadic back-and-forth exchange that becomes time consuming and inefficient. Digital discussion boards or web meeting tools such as FaceTime or WebEx are good alternatives if an in-person meeting is inconvenient.

Social Media

These days nearly everyone uses some form of social media. Some prefer Twitter or Facebook, while others use Snapchat, Instagram, or any of the countless other options. Like everything else, social media has its place in the world of communication. The biggest difference is that it can reach a huge—potentially worldwide—audience. Therein lies both its strength and its weakness.

Social media is most useful to relay a quick message to a broad audience (knowing that it may not reach everyone who might need it). Consider social media as a fill-in when other services are not available. It is advisable to use social media for less important and more general information, in part because it is an unsecure way of transmitting information. Ideally, a social media post will provide the basic need-to-know information as well as a link or reference to an e-mail or website where a more complete message can be accessed.

Avoid using social media to communicate any form of sensitive or private information. Social media is intended to be social so it is important to remember that anything you share can end up being seen by many other people. No matter how secure your privacy settings may be, the minute you share something on social media there are still ways that unintended people can still see and share it. Consider the old adage of not posting anything on social media that you wouldn't want to end up on the front page of the news.

Cloud Storage

Cloud storage makes it easy to store information away from one's personal computer or server, for use as a backup or to share data with colleagues and employees. Cloud storage is ideal for storing documents that many people need to access as a group, to gather project information, or to share notes on meetings. Depending on the features, cloud storage can be helpful for collaborative projects. However, like any tool, it has drawbacks. Organizing and keeping up with repositories can be challenging, and not all repositories support collaboration equally well. There are potential issues with security, and cloud services are generally inaccessible when an Internet connection isn't available.

Cloud storage works best if kept clean and organized. From shelves to digital spaces, everything needs to be occasionally weeded. Consider developing a policy for its use. This should include guidelines on how frequently cleanup should occur, and address the security measures available for more sensitive documents. As technology improves, there are more services available to provide a secure place to store documents.

Not all cloud storage sites provide the same services. Some are mainly storage spaces, providing little more than passive communication by allowing stored documents to be shared. If more interactive features are needed, Google Drive—although less secure—is a favorite for active and trackable collaboration. WebEx is primarily used for its streaming and video-capture abilities, offering features to share screens and documents as well as live editing. Yammer has a note feature, which provides live collaboration for up to twelve people at a time. These cloud sharing tools can be useful if greater collaboration is anticipated; if the priority is simply tracking edits, or if access and security issues are important, the classic editing capabilities in Word and sharing via group e-mail might be more suitable.

Project Management Apps

Is there anything librarians agree more on than the importance of organization? Librarians make sense out of chaos. Project management applications such as Basecamp can make management a breeze by providing calendars, document sharing, collaborative notes, and a venue for online discussion or announcements. LibCRM is a new service (still in beta at the time of this writing) from Springshare that promises to be another great tool for project management tasks and customer relations.

Project management apps are great for team projects and committee work, but can also store and track information about an individual's work goals. These tools are convenient ways for managers to keep an eye on progress. Since these apps often have a learning curve, they offer training or appoint super-users to help fully utilize their many features.

Sometimes it is best to keep things simple, especially if overlapping tools are already in use. If the team can already share appointments and deadlines in a calendar format and is successfully collaborating in a repository, then it may not be worthwhile to transfer everything over to a new application. On the other hand, if a large and complicated project looms close at hand, these management apps may be worth considering.

Continuing Education

Training is a highly specialized form of communication that can teach new procedures, explain the scope and needs of a project, or introduce new software. It can foster confidence and build camaraderie while empowering employees with the tools they need to get the job done right. Training can involve one person teaching a group or simply one person teaching another. Professionals such as librarians can be expected to learn some things on their own by seeking advice, research, and experimenting.

Managers need to be clear about the purpose of the training and how it relates to the library's strategic plan or meshes with an employee's individual goals. Sessions that are timely and relevant will provide the best outcomes; as discussed earlier, delivering information at the wrong time to the wrong audience can lead to confusion and wasted time. For sessions that run longer than about ninety minutes, be sure to offer breaks and refreshments, if possible. Training need not be boring. Mix things up by offering different types of training: some people enjoy webinars, while others prefer face-to-face sessions. Making it fun keeps everyone more engaged. It is also important to remember that while lifelong learning contributes to the success of people and institutions, training should not negatively impact workflow or cause unnecessary burden on the employees.

Conclusion

This chapter was written as a basic overview of the nature of communication and how it relates to a productive workplace, with an emphasis on understanding what the audience or recipient really needs. By using experiences at MUSC with various forms and styles of communication, including the various methods to transfer information, we hope the reader can glean some insights that can be used for good purpose in any library setting.

Note

1. "Communication," Merriam-Webster.com, accessed February 3, 2017, https://www.merriam-webster.com/dictionary/communication.

Further Reading

Basecamp website. Accessed February 3, 2017. https://basecamp.com.

Bolman, L. G., and J. V. Gallos. *Reframing Academic Leadership*. San Francisco: Jossey-Bass, 2011.

Box website. Accessed February 3, 2017. https://www.box.com.

Costello, K., and D. Del Bosque. "For Better or Worse: Using Wikis and Blogs for Staff Communication in an Academic Library." *Journal of Web Librarianship* 4 (2010): 143–60.

Facebook website. Accessed February 3, 2017. https://www.facebook.com.

"FaceTime." Mac App Store. Accessed February 3, 2017. https://itunes.apple.com/us/app/facetime/id414307850?mt=12.

Google Drive website. Accessed February 3, 2017. https://www.google.com/drive/.

Kotter, J. P. *Leading Change*. Boston: Harvard Business Review Press, 2012.

Patterson, K., J. Grenny, R. McMillan, and A. Switzler. *Crucial Conversations: Tools for Talking When Stakes Are High*. New York: McGraw-Hill Education, 2011.

Wagner, P. "The Two Sets of Contradictory Communication Rules: Maintaining Positive Performance." American Library Association website. June 26, 2010. Accessed. http://www.ala.org/lssirt/sites/ala.org.lssirt/files/content/lssirtr esources/FrontLineALAJun10.pdf.

Chapter 6

Managing Change in a Union Environment

Elaine R. Martin

The model of health sciences librarianship that has been in place for decades is being challenged. The elimination of the reference desk, the move to a single service point, the development of institutional repositories, the migration from print to electronic library, the redesign of library spaces, and the reliance on social media for communication—all indicate a dramatic change in the way libraries do business. Such trends naturally affect the roles and responsibilities professional librarians and support staff play. There already has been much written and discussed about the changing roles of the medical librarian.[1] There is a need to reexamine and redefine support staff roles. The library literature lacks materials that address the changing roles of support staff in the library in general and in medical libraries in particular, along with the managerial challenges that accompany this change.

Driven by the needs of patrons and coinciding with the trends and changes impacting libraries, some medical libraries have attempted to redefine the support staff model. A number of questions arise in developing a new model for defining, training, and promoting support staff: What are the jobs of support staff? What should the job descriptions include? What are the competencies and skills needed for these jobs? What should the compensation and promotion plan include? What is the role of unions and how can restructuring occur in a union environment? Not surprisingly, attempts to answer these questions have been met with mixed success. Some of the major themes that emerged from these restructuring efforts were: (1) unions and the ability to work with them; (2) training and the need to develop staff into their new roles; and (3) compensation and how to reward staff for taking on more responsibility, especially for those positions formerly held by librarians. Using a case study example, this chapter discusses some possible options surrounding these issues, highlights lessons learned, and concludes with tips for managers negotiating change within a unionized environment.[2]

Background

For many years, the work of library support staff has focused on inventory control, such as keeping print collections in order and keeping track of where print collections went if they left the library. It was not uncommon for support staff to shelve books, check in journals, check out books, and process print materials coming into the library as well as prepare items for the bindery. The current trends in information access, storage, and retrieval, promulgated primarily by the shift in the library's focus from print collections to digital collections, require different approaches to what support staff do.

What is the definition of support staff? In the 1970s and 1980s, it was difficult to imagine a library without support staff. Support staff often performed routine activities necessary to day-to-day library operations. Support staff work was specialized. A support staff worker was assigned to a particular department, such as technical services, where he or she performed a discrete task, such as checking in journals or ordering books. There was little crossover from one department to another, and job descriptions were distinct and simple rather than multifunctional.

Support staff titles varied, including library assistant, library clerk, and library technician. In "In the Beginning, There Was Support Staff . . . ," Edward Martinez tells the history of library support staff in the United States up to 1989.[3] Recent years of this history are charted on a time line, "Milestones of the Library Support Staff Movement," developed in an online workshop created and facilitated by Ed Gillen.[4] The time line presents highlights of library support staff development in the United States from 1971 to the present. The history shows the important role of support staff in libraries prior to the advent of new technologies and electronic resources.

Over the last twenty years, however, the amount of support staff work has declined and the line between the work done by support staff and that done by professional librarians became less distinct. Roles and responsibilities formerly performed by professionals have shifted to support staff, for example, in copy cataloging and interlibrary loan.[5] In 1989, commentators from *Library Journal* wrote, "Library support of development opportunities for all staff at all levels will be the fundamental issue of the coming decade."[6]

At the same time as these roles were changing, work in libraries became less routine. Economic challenges forced libraries to consider ways to automate and streamline daily operations. Rather than focusing on the processing of print materials, libraries began to focus on knowledge management: transmitting the information within the materials collected and transferring that knowledge to users. Skills in teaching and evaluation became more important in the knowledge-based library. The result was that the amount of work typically performed by support staff declined and in some cases disappeared entirely. One such example is in circulation. Particularly in medical libraries, given the rapid developments in scientific discovery and treatment options, the need for books has been greatly reduced. Current, up-to-date online journals have become the preferred method for information seeking and discovery. With fewer print books being purchased, coupled with automation of library circulation processes and the introduction of self-service checkout stations, fewer support staff were needed to maintain circulation desk functions. Commenting on these findings, David W. Lewis, in his 2006 article on the future of libraries, predicted a "reduction in the number of clerical positions" as a result of labor saved in managing print collections, estimating this in the range of "25% to 30% decline over the next 20 years."[7]

Complicating matters, the most recent AFL-CIO Department for Professional Employees fact sheet, "Library Workers: Facts and Figures," states that in 2015 there were 166,000 librarians compared to 129,000 library technicians and assistants in the workforce. While librarians must hold a master's degree in library science (MLS) or meet state standards to be called a librarian, technicians and assistants are not required to hold an MLS, although many have degrees in other disciplines. Overall, cumulative employment figures declined from 2007 through 2015 for both librarians and support staff, from 380,000 to 295,000. While most librarians (57 percent) worked in school and academic libraries in 2015, more than half of the library technicians and library assistants were employed by local government schools and agencies. Approximately half of all library technicians or assistants were employed part-time in 2015. Librarians and library workers are among those occupations with a high rate of unionization. Those who are in a union earn more per week than their nonunion counterparts and are more likely than their nonunion counterparts to have access to health insurance or other benefits. Therefore, collective bargaining is an important aspect of the structure of the library and its human resources component with respect to support staff. Managers often need to work in concert with the union when contemplating changes in library support staff job duties, responsibilities, and reporting.[8]

Historically, American libraries and labor groups have worked together to advocate for the free public library. This coincided with labor's concern for free public education, and the public library was viewed as a vehicle for free adult continuing education. The libraries' support of union members' lifelong learning at national and community levels was a strong motivation for organized workers to support libraries, and vice versa. The partnership that formed between libraries and unions served both the philosophical aims of libraries and the educational goals of unions. The historical underpinning of the importance of education to labor unions and the role the library plays in fostering that goal has been written about widely in library literature.[9] Understanding the importance of education to organized labor can assist a manager who needs to deal with the union when contemplating redefining the support staff model in their library.

It is important that a library embarking on a restructuring effort manage the transition purposefully and strategically. The importance of constructively working with the union at the outset of these efforts cannot be overemphasized. Support staff benefits, job descriptions, compensation, and educational opportunities are all the purview of the union and must be considered by managers contemplating a restructuring of the support staff model.[10] Using the following case study, this chapter outlines one library's program for restructuring unionized library support staff, highlights the lessons learned, and offers a set of tips for managers who need to negotiate with the union as a partner in this endeavor.

Case Study

As a result of a strategic planning initiative, the Lamar Soutter Library of the University of Massachusetts Medical School, a medium-sized academic health sciences library, embarked on a redefinition of support staff based on changes identified during the planning process. It was clear that changes in the business of library operations called for a less siloed approach to staff work assignments. Support staff were needed to move away from performing single, specialized, technical processing duties and into other areas of the library. They needed to gain expertise in many areas of the library and be rewarded for developing new skills and taking on new responsibilities. Prior to the implementation of the restructuring program, called the Levels Program, staff were assigned one job description with specific duties in one area of the library. Job descriptions were graded, and compensation was tied to grade. There was no opportunity for cross-training or promotion unless a staff member changed jobs, and the only way to change jobs was to apply for an open position in another area of the library. The issues surrounding support staff compensation, promotion, and training became the centerpiece for the library's restructuring efforts.

Elaine R. Martin

The restructuring offered support staff an opportunity to train and advance in multiple areas of library work, and to be rewarded for their efforts. The program centered around three components: education, years of service, and cross-functional training. Through a combination of these, support staff could be promoted to the next higher grade and receive a pay increase. In addition, job descriptions were standardized and rewritten based on a set of competencies identified for support staff achievement. Competencies specified the knowledge and skills that applied to all support staff. Support staff were expected to demonstrate the competencies within their assigned areas of responsibility. The evaluation process was revised to create standards for tracking and meeting goals, and each staff member maintained a personal portfolio for tracking their progress toward promotion. An extensive training program was developed to assist support staff in their new areas of responsibility and to help them achieve their competencies.

The Lamar Soutter Library support staff were members of a union. The library director and associate directors met several times with union representatives over the course of a year to develop the specifics of the program. Initial meetings outlined the need for restructuring, with presentations focusing on educating the labor relations team on what librarians did, what support staff did, how the work was changing, the changing roles of libraries, and so on. These meetings were followed by specific working sessions in which library managers presented a variety of proposals and received feedback from the union team. One member of the team was a library staff member. This was an advantage, as his support for the new program was useful in winning over the other support staff. At the outset, the union representatives responded positively to the proposed restructuring. It was clear that the program would result in a more highly educated union support staff workforce, that staff members would receive a higher base pay at the initiation of the program and opportunities for pay increases and promotions over time, and that the evaluation process for employees would be more objective, based on a framework and set of competencies.

On the other hand, there were some hurdles to overcome. The new program called for a higher minimum qualification (some college) for support staff positions, and there was some debate over the development of strong quantitative evaluation methods for measuring staff achievement toward promotion. In the end, a compromise was reached in which current employees were grandfathered in to the educational requirement and the evaluation form was accepted by all parties.

Finally, the program was launched jointly by the library director and managers with the representatives from the union during an all-staff meeting. Both groups presented aspects of the restructuring and were available for questions and answers. The team approach illustrated the union's support for the program and gave the staff confidence that their interests and concerns were being addressed. The launch was followed by celebration on both sides of the bargaining table.

Lessons Learned

There are several lessons to be learned with respect to working with the union from the Lamar Soutter Library support staff restructuring program. Managers contemplating a redefinition of their support staff model may want to apply these lessons to their own environment.

First, library management viewed the union as a partner in the restructuring effort from the outset. Meetings involved representatives from both groups who worked together to design the program. Second, the goals of the effort were not just to reassign library staff to work needed in the library, but also to provide an opportunity for union employees to learn new duties, enhance their skills, take on new responsibilities, and be fairly compensated for their work. These appealed to the historical underpinnings of organized labor in libraries. It was obvious from the outset that library management was sensitive to the needs of its labor force. Third, library management came to meetings prepared. Managers backed up their findings with data, and were prepared to listen, ask questions, and go back to do more research if necessary. Managers expected—and welcomed—questions from union representatives. Fourth, the program was developed based on strategic thinking. A yearlong strategic-planning process led to the need for a restructuring, and the program grew from identified needs resulting from that process. Fifth, the program was jointly developed by the library managers and representatives from the union, including one library support staff member. This member could communicate what was being discussed in the planning stages to the rest of the staff and bring back any staff concerns to the group. Communication within and outside of meetings, formally and informally, was key. This ongoing communication enhanced trust. As the program developed and it was clear that all support staff would receive some level of increased compensation at the beginning of the restructuring, as well as new job duties, union representatives began to trust in library management's goals for the program. Sixth, understanding the development of a restructuring takes time. It is not unusual to spend a year or more in this kind of effort. Seventh, when there was some disagreement to aspects of the initial program plan, both parties compromised, especially when it came to existing staff members. Both parties forgot about winning and losing and kept the interest of the support staff in mind.

Elaine R. Martin

Tips for Managers for Negotiating with the Union

Managers need to recognize that unionization will affect the way support staff are managed. Wages, job duties, the evaluation process, and other conditions of employment for staff are determined by the negotiation process. The following tips in negotiating with organized labor may be useful to managers contemplating a change with respect to support staff work:

- Think strategically.
- Be prepared to listen.
- Be prepared to go back to the drawing board.
- Be willing to compromise.
- Understand what is important to organized labor, and its historical under-pinnings.
- Take the time to do the work.
- Build trust.

Conclusion

Sometimes libraries view the union in an adversarial light. The Lamar Soutter Library case presents a different way of partnering with labor, based on a set of conditions that led to the joint development of a new, positive model for support staff. It may be relatively easy for today's medical library managers to dismiss the possibility of making structural changes within their library organizations because the staff are unionized. This need not be the case. In considering the lessons learned described in the case study above and the negotiating tips gleaned from the Soutter Library experience, library managers may feel better equipped to work with the union to develop a new organization.

Notes

1. Janet A. Crum and I. Diane Cooper, "Emerging Roles for Biomedical Librarians: A Survey of Current Practice, Challenges, and Changes," *Journal of the Medical Library Association* 101, no. 4 (2013): 278-86, doi: 10.3163/1536-5050.101.4.009; I. Diane Cooper and Janet A. Crum, "New Activities and Changing Roles of Health Sciences Librarians: A Systematic Review, 1990-2012," *Journal of the Medical Library Association* 101, no. 4 (2013): 268-77, doi: 10.3163/1536-5050.101.4.008; Elaine R. Martin, "Shaping Opportunities for the New Health Sciences Librarian," *Journal of the Medical Library Association* 101, no. 4 (2013): 252-53, doi: 10.3163/1536-5050.101.4.004; Jane Fama and Elaine Martin, "One Model for Creating a Career Ladder for Library Support Staff," *Journal of Academic Leadership* (2009) 35, no. 5: 475-81: doi: 10.1016/j.acalib.2009.06.018.
2. Jane Fama et al., "Level Program Report: Lamar Soutter Library," 2007. Internal Report of the Lamar Soutter Library, University of Massachusetts Medical School, Worcester, MA. Case study, print.

3. Edward B. Martinez, "In the Beginning, There Was Support Staff . . . ," American Library Association website, 1989, accessed August 7, 2016, http://www.ala.org/offices/hrdr/librarysupportstaff/history_of_library_support_staff.
4. "Milestones of the Library Support Staff Movement," American Library Association website, 1996, accessed August 7, 2016, http://www.ala.org/offices/hrdr/library supportstaff/milestones_of_the_library_support_staff_movement.
5. American Library Association, "American Library Association Office for Library Personnel Resources Standing Committee on Library Education," Issue Paper #9, September 17, 1991, accessed August 7, 2016, http://www.ala.org/educationcareers/educa tion/3rdcongressonpro/roledefinition.
6. "Career Development: Defining the 'Issues of the Nineties,'" Library Journal 114, no. 12 (1989): 52.
7. David W. Lewis, "A Strategy for Academic Libraries in the First Quarter of the 21st Century," College & Research Libraries 68 no. 5 (2007): 418, doi: 10.5860/crl.68.5.418.
8. "Library Workers: Facts & Figures," Department for Professional Employees website, 2016, http://dpeaflcio.org/programs-publications/issue-fact-sheets/library-work ers-facts-figures.
9. Kathleen de la Peña McCook, "Unions in Public and Academic Libraries," University of South Florida School of Information Faculty Publications, paper 108 (2010), accessed December 2016, http://scholarcommons.usf.edu/si_facpub/108; Arthur S. Meyers, "Building a Partnership: Library Service to Labor," American Libraries 30, no. 7 (1999): 52–55, accessed July 13, 2016, http://www.jstor.org/stable/25637247.
10. Rachel Applegate, "Who Benefits? Unionization and Academic Libraries and Librarians," Library Quarterly: Information, Community, Policy 79, no. 4 (2009): 443–63, accessed July 8, 2016, http://www.jstor.org/stable/10.1086/605383.

Elaine R. Martin

Chapter 7

Knowing and Understanding the Staff

Dixie Jones

As services and technologies evolve, the functions of medical library staff change along with them. In today's budgetary environment, when labor demands rise, administrators cannot always afford to create new positions; they must rely on their current staff. Now more than ever, library managers need to know their employees—their personalities, work styles, motivations, strengths, and weaknesses—in order to use them most effectively. With this knowledge, libraries can do more with less, and meet new and challenging demands head-on. This chapter explores several avenues managers can use to more fully understand the abilities of their staff, including examples derived from the author's own library.

The prescribed tasks within a position are less rigid than they were in the past. This fluidity or openness can be used to advantage by the library in meeting the evolving needs of its clientele. A new task may be added to an employee's duties without necessarily involving human resources (unless a union is present and requires a formal action). The additional duties needn't be piled onto existing work, but can be a replacement for work that now takes up less time, has been abandoned, or has become a lower priority. The processing of physical books is one obvious example of a task that now demands less time. Tasks such as these have been transformed as emphasis has shifted from print to digital. Managers need to be aware of what each employee does in his or her day-to-day work, as circumstances dictate that some tasks be changed, added, or dropped on a more frequent basis.

Few libraries can afford to have a full-time position for every duty. For example, a library might need a coordinator for educational efforts who is not involved with actual teaching duties. This position can be part-time, using full-time librarians for instruction for their liaison departments as well as for general classes. Liaison duties should reflect particular knowledge and skill sets; for example, someone who has experience in a laboratory setting might be a good fit for a liaison position with the Department of Clinical Laboratory Science. Position descriptions need not be specific as to what department liaison duties fall under. Liaison assignments can change, of course, but if a liaison has been working successfully with a department for a long time, replacing him or her with another librarian—even one who has more appropriate experience—may not be advantageous.

An employee's knowledge and skills can be identified through testing, annual evaluations, observation, and discussion with other staff members. Library managers must be alert to a staff member's actual expertise, even when it doesn't match his or her credentials. An employee may not possess a MLS degree, for example, but still be effective in helping customers find the information they need. Managers should not discount these abilities, nor should they be in the dark about other hidden or underutilized skills a staff member may possess. Kimberley Bugg notes that

> developing human capital that is appropriate for a particular library is not an exact science. The art of matching the roles and responsibilities of a library position within an institution of higher education with a potential candidate is a complicated task, especially considering the rapidly shifting priorities of the academic library. For that reason, academic libraries should apply talent acquisition strategies that focus on finding individuals that best fit the organizational culture rather than a particular position.[1]

This thinking differs from conventional practices, when a manager's goal was to hire someone whose education and skills more precisely matched the position's duties. It places greater emphasis on soft skills and personality—the assumption being that an intelligent, motivated employee can learn, or be trained, to do anything. With this in mind, a manager should not only be cognizant of these traits in the current staff, but look at potential new hires' abilities in such things as "basic electronic skills, ability to teach, negotiation skills, and experience solving problems."[2]

While new graduates may possess ready-made skills suited for the twenty-first century, experienced staff can learn new skills as well. When planning to offer a new service that does not fall into anyone's usual domain, a manager's knowledge of his or her staff is crucial. Perhaps there is someone on staff who already has an aptitude or some experience related to the new service or is willing to adjust his or her duties and take on a new challenge. Staff development and training for a new service will be discussed later, but is applicable here because someone needs to be willing to acquire knowledge and skills to offer the new service.

"In order to match staff with redefined organizational priorities, it is necessary to determine who is doing what currently."[3] Knowing the staff's day-to-day duties well, the library director can identify whether or not time is being wasted on tasks that are outdated or of low priority. "This is how it's always been done" is not good enough anymore. Analysis of tasks can provide an opportunity to start doing things that better mesh with current priorities. If training or education is needed, it should be provided, either internally or externally. Change can produce anxieties, but assuring staff they will be properly trained for new tasks helps alleviate fears and engender confidence. Human resources can provide guidance on changing responsibilities, as well as determining whether they are significant enough to require changes in position descriptions and performance plans.[4]

Generic or soft skills can be incorporated into position descriptions. These skills—nonspecific to particular duties, but which can be broadly applied—include,

Writing Service: Students at the library were asking for assistance in writing personal statements and papers. The school has no such service. Two librarians on staff with writing credentials offered to start a writing service. They consulted with library administration, who gave the service a blessing, and the two librarians set guidelines. The service was advertised through the library's usual communications channels, and it took off right away. Those two staff members have since left to take jobs elsewhere, but other staff members have stepped up and volunteered to assist with this burgeoning service. Students, residents, and faculty submit requests through a group e-mail account created for the writing consultants. The services provided expanded to include the editing of manuscripts submitted for publication. Residents and faculty members for whom English is a second language have been particularly grateful for the service. Guidelines have been tweaked as necessary. There are now four library staff members serving as writing consultants, in addition to performing their usual duties. The service is very popular and has filled a niche, but it has almost become a victim of its own success. Discussions are being held about whether to reduce the number of writing jobs accepted or recruit more staff members to assist with the service. As with any service, there must be enough manpower to avoid overburdening staff.

"problem-solving, critical thinking, effective communication, teamwork and ethical thinking."[5] When hiring, managers should look for these attributes as much as function-related skills. While this chapter focuses on knowing and understanding current staff members, determining who has these attributes when hiring is an important part of the process of assembling an effective team. Taking the time to discern whether or not interviewees have these generic skills is time well spent.

Most libraries are seeing staffing changes in response to the transformation of information resources from print to electronic formats. As fewer serials need to be checked in, claimed, or sent to the bindery, and as fewer materials require physical processing, managers must proactively deal with the shuffling of duties. Employees who have had their work reduced because of this may have skills or interests that can be applied to other duties. For example, a cataloging assistant with an interest (or perhaps a degree) in history can assist with processing materials for the archives or with digitizing historical materials so they can be made available online. Employees who don't have the skills suitable for today's electronic environment need training. New duties for nonprofessionals might include PubMed LinkOut holdings updates, link resolver work, link checking, IP management, or troubleshooting of access problems.[6]

As library duties expand into nontraditional areas to meet institutional needs, hiring practices will also have to be less traditional, with more use of "feral professionals."[7] Feral library employees are described as those who have advanced degrees in fields other than library science or possess special skills such as information technology. Library managers must be able to distinguish between duties that can be handled by traditional library staff and duties that are better performed by nonlibrarians who have specialized skill sets.

When hiring new staff, managers may decide to settle for fewer hard skills in order to get someone who has the potential to mesh well with the library and its staff.[8] People can learn new skills more easily than they can change their personalities or earn new degrees. David W. Lewis notes that library managers use the master of library science (MLS) degree as a filter when, according to him, it is not clear that what is taught in the degree program is related to the needs of an academic library.[9] The MLS degree does not guarantee the soft, generic traits or skills needed in academic libraries: things such as honesty, even temperament, flexibility, initiative, and ability to cooperate with teams and serve diverse populations. In essence, the library director may find it worth considering a non-MLS candidate when hiring for a position.

When an emerging and novel task demands attention, choosing the right person is important, because this person will become a trailblazer. If the "experiment" is a success, it can lead to the creation of a new position, funded either by the library budget or another department's budget. If a new position is out of the question, a team can be created to disperse the workload among its members. Deborah A. Carver notes, "As academic libraries face increased competition for funding within their institutions, the ability to demonstrate the library's contribution to the research and teaching missions becomes more critical. Large research libraries often have staff devoted exclusively to the collection and analysis of data, but it may be more common for libraries to appoint a team of individuals who take on this assignment in addition to their regular responsibilities."[10]

Understanding Generational Differences in Staff Members

"Generations, like people, have personalities."[11] In understanding the workforce, library managers must take into account the generational mix. The literature on generational differences is abundant, and some may argue that the year of one's birth does not determine success in the library profession. However, it cannot be denied that younger employees in the profession grew up in a much different world than that of earlier generations. Being familiar with the attributes of each generation can be helpful in matching projects or duties with particular people. Since Generation X (born between 1964 and 1984) is smaller than either the Baby Boomer generation (born between 1946 and 1964) or the Millennial generation (also known as Generation Y; born between 1984 and 2004), there are fewer of them to step into leadership roles as Boomers retire. Poor retention of Gen X librarians "will clearly exacerbate an already impending library staffing shortage."[12]

Library managers need to know what makes Gen X employees tick in order to retain them. A 2005 survey of new librarians "found that 69% had voluntarily switched jobs or roles within their first five years in the profession" and "half of the nearly 500 survey respondents reported that they were considering leaving the library profession altogether."[13] Mentoring is one way to improve retention rates. Librarians in the 2005 study asserted that mentoring contributed to job satisfaction. Catherine Bloomquist offers several alternatives to the traditional mentoring model of older to younger pairing, such as reverse mentoring, bidirectional mentoring, progressive mentoring, and peer mentoring.[14] Talking to Gen X employees about these options can be helpful in determining what kind of mentoring to offer them. As Boomers retire, new librarians who have been exposed to mentoring may be better equipped to step into leadership roles.

Meanwhile, Millennials have surpassed Boomers as America's largest generation. New immigrants to the United States are more likely to be members of the Millennial generation than the Boomer generation, and there are fewer Boomers immigrating to the United States than there are native-born Boomers passing away.[15] Generation X dominated the workforce for only three years, ending in 2015, when Millennials became predominant.[16] Managers should become familiar with the general traits associated with Millennials and provide an environment that attracts them: "The tendency to think out of the box, try new things, work hard, be ambitious, work collaboratively, and not follow tradition, solely because it's tradition, are some of this generation's habits that management should recognize."[17] However, a Pew report states that "[o]f the four generations [Millennial, Gen X, Boomer, Silent], Millennials are the only one that doesn't cite 'work ethic' as one of their principal claims to distinctiveness."[18] They are the digital natives who have grown up online and are accustomed to ubiquitous technology.[19] Flexibility may be more important to them than in previous generations. Library managers might be limited by institutional regulations regarding work hours, but there are usually some ways in which a degree of flexibility can be offered. Millennials appreciate positive feedback, work-life balance, and loads of recognition. Libraries should offer these workplace attributes in order to keep Millennials engaged.[20] As Les Pickett notes, "Millennials whose needs for support, appreciation and flexibility are not met are more likely to leave a workplace."[21] They want a workplace that emphasizes teamwork and a sense of community. They want to have input on their assigned tasks and need continuing support from their supervisors. Pickett recommends managing employees on a personal level with an eye toward individual needs and preferences, and knowing generational differences can help in that endeavor.

Kerry Keegan notes that Millennials and Baby Boomers share some commonalities apart from Generation X, which is sandwiched between them: "Library administrations can take advantage of the unique knowledge sets of these two factions through peer-to-peer cross-training."[22] Millennials get along well with others, especially their elders.[23] Both Boomers and Millennials thrive in cooperative environments, and "administrators will be pleasantly surprised at the parallels in their work ethics and learning preferences. Workplaces that take advantage of these overlaps through appropriate instructional and team-building exercises will benefit from the dedication to community and success shown by both groups."[24] Millennials can teach older generations about technology; conversely, Boomers and Generation Xers in management positions can teach Millennials interpersonal, administrative, and managerial skills.[25] Managers should facilitate this shared learning for the benefit of their libraries.

While Millennial library science graduates are comfortable with use of technology, they are not necessarily skilled in programming or creating complex websites. Jenny Emanuel conducted a survey of Millennial library school students and library science graduates. Respondents indicated their comfort levels with specified types of technology before and after library school, and at the present time. Generally, they were not comfortable with the information architecture

Dixie Jones

Marketing through Social Media: Every medical library practices marketing to some degree. Traditionally, this has been done via a newsletter (print or electronic), flyers, web postings, and, more recently, digital bulletin boards. Libraries market via different media in order to reach more patrons. While not all staff members possess an interest in or aptitude for using social media, it is likely there exists someone who does. When a younger-generation librarian joined the staff, she volunteered to assist with social media (Facebook and Twitter) as a marketing/communication tool and to write guidelines for their use.

skills CSS and HTML. They also lacked knowledge of relational databases such as Linux, C++, ASP, and PERL. The most popular skill they wanted to learn was programming. While Millennials have grown up using various forms of technology, library managers cannot assume they all have advanced technical skills, such as those needed to build databases.[26] Unless they have systems training, Millennials might be better suited to softer technology skills, such as managing the library's Facebook page. Once considered a leisure activity (and sometimes even banned at work), Facebook has become a staple for marketing library activities, resources, and events.

Millennials value meaningful work that offers personal satisfaction. They like to know that they are making a difference.[27] A supervisor needs to explain to a Millennial how his or her job contributes to the library as a whole. Understanding the importance of a job motivates an employee. Millennial employees want to grow and move upward. While supervisors might not be able to promote all Millennials (such as student workers), they can help them learn new skills and assign new duties to keep them engaged. Whatever managers can do to help employees feel they are moving forward can increase job satisfaction and retention.[28]

In a survey of library student workers at Brigham Young University (BYU), several students mentioned that they had trouble understanding or following instructions from their supervisors (assumed to be older); others said they had difficulty explaining problems to their supervisors, especially regarding technology. One survey commentator stated, "[I]t's often apparent that our supervisor doesn't understand what we are trying to say because they're not as familiar with tech jargon. . . . I can easily explain a problem I'm having to a fellow Millennial coworker, but my supervisor doesn't quite grasp it."[29] Understanding the reasons behind problems between different generations of staff members can be the first step toward avoiding or solving them. Library managers can encourage younger and older workers to make an effort to communicate so they are understood by each other. Expectations about phone calls, text messages, and dress standards should be spelled out up front so that everyone is on the same page and conflict can be avoided.[30]

The BYU survey and Pew studies indicate that work ethic is not the defining value or characteristic of Millennials—they concede that older generations work harder. As noted by Sara D. Smith and Quinn Galbraith, this does not mean they do not work hard. They are more motivated by factors such as flexibility, meaningful work, relationships with their supervisors, and growth opportunities than by a traditional work ethic.[31] Motivated by a desire to please, they want feedback from supervisors about how they are doing and how they can do better. Millennials are harder on themselves than their supervisors are: "For example, 28% of students said Millennials are lazy, 54% said they are self-centered, and 71% said they feel entitled; however, only 9%, 20%, and 4% (respectively) of supervisors felt these terms described the Millennial Generation."[32] Smith and Galbraith explain that supervisors should understand the importance of encouraging and mentoring Millennials, helping them overcome negative stereotypes. They want to be recognized for their successes on an ongoing basis. Regular communication about how they are doing is a motivator for them. Library managers "need to better understand this generation . . . in order to recruit, retain, and motivate new staff members who will gradually replace the Baby Boomers."[33]

Knowing What Motivates Staff Members

A report from the Society for Human Resource Management's 2015 Employee Job Satisfaction and Engagement Survey found that 88 percent of employees were satisfied with their jobs, with the most important contributor being "respectful treatment of all employees at all levels."[34] If a manager sees an employee losing interest or becoming disengaged, the solution might be to work with him or her on finding new responsibilities that better match his or her interests or abilities. As Sarah Cook points out, "To foster long-term, sustained motivation, recent thought is that managers must inspire employees to draw their motivation from inside rather than rely on external factors such as pay."[35] R. David Lankes further notes that "The key as an organization is to find out what motivates an individual and create conditions that match that innovation."[36] In a cohort study involving library science students, it was found that "engagement in the work (intrinsic motivation—34%) was the prevailing motivator in three out of four cohorts," as shown in figure 7.1.[37]

As previously discussed, awareness of the traits associated with different generations can help library managers understand what motivates each generation. According to Lisa Kurt, Millennials "often make little distinction between

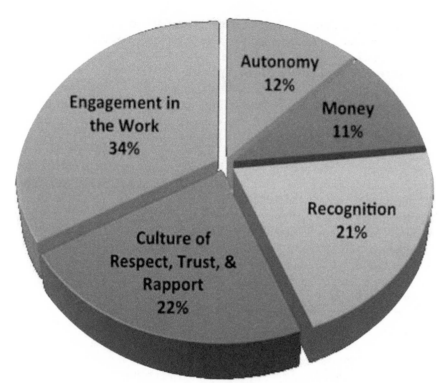

Figure 7.1. Summary of extrinsic and intrinsic motivators in four student cohorts.

work and play."[38] Knowing how play can be incorporated into productivity and creativity is an important asset for library managers: "Play is a powerful method of fostering creativity and innovation in organizations."[39] If library directors wish to inspire their staff members to innovate, they must provide an environment that motivates them to do so, and this can mean bringing a spirit of play into the picture. Kurt notes that "while libraries are growing increasingly sensitive to the importance of playful environments for users, less attention is paid to providing playful environments for library employees."[40] Kurt, Sarah Cook, and Daniel H. Pink agree that managers should depend on intrinsic motivation, rather than reward and punishment, to help employees stay engaged in their work.[41] Kim Leeder writes of the psychology of play, believing it "opens our minds," helping us to resolve daily issues: "In libraries, where greater innovation is sorely needed to improve systems and embrace dramatic changes in the information landscape, play could be the key to ensuring a vibrant, relevant future."[42]

Library managers should be careful not to assume the younger generation will be the most successful at innovation. R. David Lankes notes that some library managers hire new grads to be the innovators in their libraries, assuming they are always familiar with the latest technology. He observes that some library directors place innovation with their least experienced person, who has less knowledge of the institution and fewer political skills. His argument is not that new hires should be excluded, but rather that successful innovation requires involvement by librarians with a mix of experience.[43]

Rajesh Singh notes, "The concepts of extrinsic and intrinsic motivators are not only important for individual performance, but they also play a critical role in influencing the performance of teams in a project or organization and worth exploring for managers in information organizations."[44] Pink advocates putting together diverse teams whose members are different enough from one another to provide stimulation.[45] Leslie Yerkes, like Pink, believes that diversity brings stimulation. Understanding that concept can help a library director put together more creative and effective teams: "When everyone is encouraged to bring of themselves, to offer up their glorious differences, then our feast becomes rich in texture, quality, substance, nuance, and most of all—fun!"[46] Pink advises against spurring team members to compete with one another—this, he says, undermines intrinsic motivation.[47] "Competitiveness is a major hindrance to collegiality. It fosters mistrust and professional jealousy."[48] Members of teams are motivated by having a shared mission or purpose. According to Kenneth W. Thomas, a "compelling shared purpose transforms the relationships between team members—including the relationship between you, as the leader, and the rest of the team."[49]

Applying these principles can be as simple as allowing people who like working together on projects to team up. They may develop a synergistic relationship and enjoy the camaraderie of sharing a creative mission. The quality of the work they produce can only be enriched by this. "Understanding what motivators work best in a given situation is key to motivating information professionals at individual, team, and organizational levels."[50] Library managers need to understand that when work is both fulfilling and fun, library staff members will want to stay: "The integration of fun with work creates a natural-attraction force that is irresistible to good people. Discover the secret to success: hire good people and get out of their way."[51]

Assessing Talents and Skills of Staff

Library managers generally hire people whose education and experience match the requirements of the position. However, as discussed earlier, position descriptions are more fluid now, and library duties are rapidly evolving away from traditional tasks. Staff members find themselves wearing many hats in order to meet the goals of the library and its parent institution. Having a variety of

Community Outreach: Smaller medical libraries may not have enough resources to dedicate a full position to community outreach. One library has
a position for coordinating education and outreach, but that staff member
does not personally do all the teaching or outreach; instead, outreach activities are dispersed throughout the staff. Several staff members teamed
up to apply for funding for a health information literacy project to create
a comic book on healthy habits. Two of them wrote the comic book and
contracted with a local university student to create the illustrations. The
pediatrics department provided funding to print more copies of the comic
book once the project was complete; the comic book is also available
online. One of the two librarians initiated a series of story hours at public
libraries. Each story hour focuses on a particular health topic and includes
interactive activities in addition to hearing the book. The staff members
were very engaged in these outreach functions, which were not part of
their regular job duties but which provided a service to the community,
assisting with the outreach goal of the institution.

duties can be beneficial, as long as the total workload is not overwhelming;
most people welcome duties that fit their talents and interests, and having multiple responsibilities can forestall the boredom that comes with the repetitive
nature of many library tasks. For example, a staff member who enjoys (but is
not primarily responsible for) technology may like operating a makerspace that
includes teaching people how to use a 3-D printer. Admittedly, these opportunities may not be available in libraries with large staffs, and may also not be
possible in a setting such as a small hospital library.

Employee résumés may emphasize only those skills required for their position.
Gary Fitsimmons points out that employees may have other useful skills, such
as mechanical aptitude with office equipment or fluency in a second language.
To keep up with the varied skills of staff, library managers can maintain databases or spreadsheets. Knowing what staff members have skills that relate to
neceesary tasks facilitates assigning appropriate functions to staff members.
Fitsimmons writes,

This requires thinking of your job description as being as fluid as those who
fill them. In this model, the tasks are constant, but how they are combined to
form each job description changes (not usually drastically) each time you add
any new skill or set of skills to the mix through a current or new staff member.
Thinking this way in turn requires that you (and your staff) be willing to try new
things and new combinations of tasks under each position description. This is

Electronic Health Records: Offering evidence-based electronic resources through the electronic health record (EHR) is a mostly twenty-first-century development in health sciences libraries. It is now an area of collaboration beween library staff, IT personnel, clinical personnel, and resource vendors. A subset is working with MedlinePlus Connect in the related personal health records for patients. The library must identify who on its staff is best suited for this; it may be a library systems person, a collection management librarian, a reference person/clinical medical librarian, or an administrator. Any person with some interest and time can be the one to collaborate with other departments to integrate literature into the EHR, even though it is not likely to be in anyone's official position description.

difficult because people do not like change, but it can be facilitated by proposing changes before making them, diligently soliciting staff input, and taking into consideration as much as possible any strong objections that they may have to proposed changes. Once again, if they feel they have a say in the process they are much more likely to accept changes with a good attitude, and feeling that their talents and skills are being put to good use helps as well. Each new hire or skill realignment should be seen as an opportunity for improving the balance in the workload distribution among your staff members. . . . If a function does not seem to be working in one department, look around for a better fit for it. . . . Staff should be encouraged to view minor tweaking of functions as a normal, ongoing part of their jobs, with the understanding they prevent major shakeups from happening as often and that once things come into balance they will stay that way for a least a reasonable period of time.[52]

One way to determine each staff member's strengths is to test people using a standardized instrument. One library system used a test called the Strengths-Finder Profile, refined by Gallup over a period of forty years. This instrument provides a ranked list of thirty-four traits or talents that can highlight an individual's work personality. A trainer for the library group observed that the test is practical and works well with professionals such as librarians. Teresa L. Jacobsen outlines five implications for libraries in applying strength assessment: succession planning, project planning, team building, staff appreciation, and personal development awareness. She suggests a review of an employee's strengths chart prior to annual evaluation, which allows the supervisor and employee to work together in writing at least one performance goal that relies on that employee's strengths.[53] This suggestion seems to be a win-win strategy that motivates and encourages the staff member, provides the supervisor-employee relationship craved by millennials, and promotes good outcomes for the library.

Karolien Selhorst writes, "Libraries excel in managing information and knowledge captured in books and documents, but they fail in locating and managing the knowledge potential in the heads of their own people." She advocates conducting a "knowledge audit" to help determine who has what type of knowledge, and what knowledge can be applied to advance library goals. Her library utilized an online survey followed by individual interviews to unearth the hidden talents of staff members. They determined that they could use a wiki as an accessible place to store the knowledge profiles of staff members, including lists of skills, knowledge, hobbies, and previous experiences.[54]

Onboarding programs, usually thought of as a means to acclimate new hires to an organization, can also serve to acquaint the organization with new employees' personalities as well as their general abilities. Published research indicates that some new employees place value on being recognized for who they are, i.e., affirmation of their beliefs about themselves which results in improved onboarding and long-term performance. Bruce Keisling and Melissa Laning interviewed academic librarians who had served less than two years in their positions. One-third of those interviewed indicated that library administrators getting to know them would lead to "greater alignment of their strengths with organizational objectives."[55] A small number mentioned administration of a standardized personal inventory, such as StrengthsFinder 2.0. Obviously, library managers cannot immediately know all the strengths of their new employees, but whether these strengths are determined through a test instrument or in-depth conversations, finding out about skills and interests can be beneficial for all involved.

Dejun Tony Kong and Violet T. Ho state that individual strengths can be measured, developed, and effectively managed for performance improvement. They have validated the relevance of studying employee strengths by demonstrating positive performance outcomes. They write that managers "may find it productive to design or allocate work responsibilities based on employees'strengths."[56] Directing these strengths toward duties that will move the library toward its goals is a win for the library and for the employee in terms of job satisfaction.

"Everyone is different; this uniqueness of personality and talent is not a negative factor in pulling together toward a common goal when these talents are effectively used and people are given tasks which match their abilities and interests."[57]

Conclusion

New needs continually arise in health science institutions, and libraries can assist with meeting those needs. Being fully aware of staff members' personalities as well as their knowledge, experiences, and talents, library managers will be better armed to meet new challenges. Getting to know staff members is well worth the effort and can add a layer of richness to their interactions with management and with one another.

Notes

1. Kimberley Bugg, "Best Practices for Talent Acquisition in 21st-Century Academic Libraries," *Library Leadership & Management* 29 (2015): 1–14.
2. Bryan S. Vogh, "Opportunities and Challenges for Libraries: An Open Letter," *College & Undergraduate Libraries* 18 (2011): 99.
3. Michael A. Crumpton, "Strategic Positioning for Staff Realignment," *Bottom Line* 25 (2012): 144.
4. Ibid.
5. Biddy Fisher, Gillian Hallam, and Helen Partridge, "Different Approaches: Common Conclusions. The Skills Debate of the Twenty-First Century," *New Review of Academic Librarianship* 11 (2005): 16.
6. Sarah Glasser, "Disappearing Jobs: Staffing Implications for Print Serials Management," *Serials Review* 36 (2010): 138–46.
7. John Edge and Ravonne Green, "The Graying of Academic Librarians: Crisis or Revolution?" *Journal of Access Services* 8 (2011): 97–106; James G. Neal, "Raised by Wolves: Integrating the New Generation of Feral Professionals into the Academic Library," *Library Journal* 131 (2006): 42–44; Jake R. Carlson and Jeremy R. Garritano, "E-Science, Cyberinfrastructure and the Changing Face of Scholarship," in *The Expert Library: Staffing, Sustaining, and Advancing the Academic Library in the 21st Century*, ed. Scott Walter and Karen Williams, 234–69 (Chicago: Association of College and Research Libraries, 2010).
8. Gary Fitsimmons, "Functioning Staff or Staffing Functions?" *Bottom Line: Managing Library Finances* 25 (2012): 152–54.
9. David W. Lewis, "Academic Library Staffing a Decade from Now," In *The Expert Library: Staffing, Sustaining, and Advancing the Academic Library in the 21st Century*, ed. Scott Walter and Karen Williams, 1–29 (Chicago: Association of College and Research Libraries, 2010).
10. Deborah A. Carver, 2010. "Organizational Models and Roles," *Journal of Access Services* 7 (2010): 82.
11. Pew Research Center, "Millennials: Confident. Connected. Open to Change," executive summary, February 24, 2010, accessed September 25, 2016, http://www.pew socialtrends.org/2010/02/24/millennials-confident-connected-open-to-change.
12. Catherine Bloomquist, "Mentoring Gen-X Librarians," *Public Libraries* 53 (2014): 30.
13. Ibid., 31.
14. Ibid.
15. Richard Fry, "Millennials Overtake Baby Boomers as America's Largest Generation," Pew Research Center, April 25, 2016, accessed August 12, 2016, http://www.pew research.org/fact-tank/2016/04/25/millennials-overtake-baby-boomers.
16. Richard Fry, "Millennials Surpass Gen Xers as the Largest Generation in U.S. Labor Force," Pew Research Center, May 11, 2015, accessed August 12, 2016, http://www

.pewresearch.org/fact-tank/2015/05/11/millennials-surpass-gen-xers-as-the-larg est-generation-in-u-s-labor-force.

17. Shannon Gordon, "Once You Get Them, How Do You Keep Them? Millennial Librarians at Work," *New Library World* 111 (2010): 394.

18. Pew Research Center. 2010. "Millennials: Confident.Connected. Open to Change." Executive Summary. Accessed September 25, 2016. http://www.pewsocialtrends .org/2010/02/24/millennials-confident-connected-open-to-change/.

19. Bugg, "Best Practices for Talent Acquisition in 21st-Century Academic Libraries"; Jenny Emanuel, "Digital Native Librarians, Technology Skills, and Their Relationship with Technology," *Information Technology and Libraries* 32 (2013): 20-33.

20. Bugg, "Best Practices for Talent Acquisition in 21st-Century Academic Libraries."

21. Les Pickett, "Evolving Talent Strategy to Match the Millennial Workforce Reality." *Training & Development* 40 (2013): 14.

22. Kerry Keegan, "X, Y and Z Are Call Numbers, Not Co-workers: Communicating through Generational Differences," *Feliciter* 27 (2011): 222.

23. Pew Research Center, "Millennials: Confident. Connected. Open to Change."

24. Keegan, "X, Y and Z Are Call Numbers, Not Co-workers: Communicating through Generational Differences," 222.

25. Edge and Green, "The Graying of Academic Librarians."

26. Fry, "Millennials Overtake Baby Boomers as America's Largest Generation."

27. Edge and Green, "The Graying of Academic Librarians"; Sara D. Smith and Quinn Galbraith, "Motivating Millennials: Improving Practices in Recruiting, Retaining, and Motivating Younger Library Staff," *Journal of Academic Librarianship* 38 (2012): 135-44.

28. Smith and Galbraith, "Motivating Millennials."

29. Ibid., 140.

30. Ibid.

31. Ibid.

32. Ibid., 142.

33. Ibid., 143.

34. "All the Happy People," *TD: Talent Development* (July 1, 2016): 15.

35. Sarah Cook, *The Essential Guide to Employee Engagement: Better Business Performance through Staff Satisfaction* (Philadelphia: Kogan Page, 2008), 85.

36. R. David Lankes, "Innovators Wanted: No Experience Necessary?" In *The Expert Library: Staffing, Sustaining, and Advancing the Academic Library in the 21st Century*, ed. Scott Walter and Karen Williams, 52-75 (Chicago: Association of College and Research Libraries, 2010), 70.

37. Rajesh Singh, "The Impact of Intrinsic and Extrinsic Motivators on Employee Engagement in Information Organizations," *Journal of Education for Library and Information Science* 7 (2016): 202.

38. Lisa Kurt, William Kurt, and Ann Medaille, "The Power of Play: Fostering Creativity and Innovation in Libraries," *Journal of Library Innovation* 1 (2010): 10.

39. Ibid., 8.

40. Ibid., 12.

41. Cook, *The Essential Guide to Employee Engagement*; Kurt, Kurt, and Medaille, "The Power of Play"; Daniel H. Pink, *Drive: The Surprising Truth about What Motivates Us* (New York: Riverhead Books, 2009).

42. Kim Leeder, "The Play Time Manifesto: Why Having Fun Makes Us Better Workers. Let's Play!" *Journal of Library Administration* 54 (2014): 625.
43. Lankes, "Innovators Wanted."
44. Singh, "The Impact of Intrinsic and Extrinsic Motivators on Employee Engagement in Information organizations," *Journal of Education for Library and Information Science* 7 (2016): 200.
45. Pink, *Drive*.
46. Leslie Yerkes, *Fun Works: Creating Places Where People Love to Work*, 2nd ed. (San Francisco: Berrett-Koehler, 2007), 77.
47. Pink, *Drive*.
48. Dixie A. Jones, "Plays Well with Others, or the Importance of Collegiality within a Reference Unit," *Reference Librarian* 59 (1997): 169.
49. Kenneth W. Thomas, *Intrinsic Motivation at Work: What Really Drives Employee Engagement*, 2nd ed. (San Francisco: Berrett-Koehler, 2009), 27.
50. Singh, "The Impact of Intrinsic and Extrinsic Motivators on Employee Engagement in Information Organizations," 198.
51. Yerkes, *Fun Works*, 139.
52. Fitsimmons, "Functioning Staff or Staffing Functions?," 153.
53. Teresa L. Jacobsen, "Showing Our Strengths" *Library Journal* 13 (2010): 28–31.
54. Karolien Selhorst, "Knowledge Management: Making Use of Hidden Staff Talent," *Library + Information Update* 7 (2008): 38.
55. Bruce Keisling and Melissa Laning, "We Are Happy to Be Here: The Onboarding Experience in Academic Libraries." *Journal of Library Administration* 56 (2016): 388.
56. Dejun Tony Kong and Violet T. Ho, "A Self-Determination Perspective of Strengths Use at Work: Examining its Determinant and Performance Implications," *Journal of Positive Psychology* 11 (2016): 23.
57. Jones, "Plays Well with Others," 166.

Chapter 8

Working at the Speed of Scale

Gerald Perry and Michael Brewer

In early 2016, Klaus Schwab, founder and executive chairman of the World Economic Forum (WEF), published the book *The Fourth Industrial Revolution*. What is the fourth industrial? According to the WEF website dedicated to the publication, it is "[u]biquitous, mobile supercomputing. Intelligent robots. Self-driving cars. Neuro-technological brain enhancements. Genetic editing." It is an entirely new, transformational shift from what has been called the Information Age to what Schwab describes as "the brink of a technological revolution that will fundamentally alter the way we work, and relate to one another. In its scale, scope and complexity, the transformation will be unlike anything humankind has experienced before." Whence the hyperbole? According to Schwab, "The possibilities of billions of people connected by mobile devices, with unprecedented processing power, storage capacity, and access to knowledge, are unlimited. And these possibilities will be multiplied by emerging technology breakthroughs in fields such as artificial intelligence, robotics, the Internet of Things, autonomous vehicles, 3-D printing, nanotechnology, materials science, energy storage, and quantum computing."[1]

What Schwab is describing here at a macro level is in fact being experienced, at least in fits and starts, at the micro level in our academic libraries. At the University of Arizona Libraries (UAL), where the authors work, we have launched what we call the iSpace, a local iteration of the popular library-based makerspace. We support 3-D printing at both our Main and Health Sciences libraries. We check out and support technology-enhanced learning for faculty and students across disciplines in this space, with items such as Google Cardboard,

Oculus Rift, and Raspberry Pi, among others.² Our vision is one of providing broad and ubiquitous access to information resources and technologies in as wide a range of formats and configurations as is feasible.

These efforts are largely posited on a progressive, service-oriented vision of academic librarianship, where the client is seen as central to the mission and innovation is a core strategy in service to that mission. The UAL Strategic Plan articulates as our first strategy in service to campus the commitment to "[d]esign and implement innovative programming and provide extraordinary content to advance learning, research, and community impact."³ Our efforts toward advancing this mission embrace the promise of delivering information resources and services, as well as contemporary technologies, affordably at scale, informed by the belief that in so doing UAL is contributing to advancing student success largely conceived as agility in the economic marketplace, creating a service context for technology-enabled research and discovery, and facilitating network-informed connections between people. Fundamental to this orientation is an appreciation for what it means to be a transformed academic library, leveraging the advances of digital information and processing tools as meaningful "library as service" resources to a twenty-first-century university campus.⁴

Scale and Its Implications

The promise of scale is central to the success of the innovations we champion; this scale, made possible by the digital revolution, now defines much of what we do. Emerging tools for knowledge acquisition, application, and discovery are all enabled by scale, including learning analytics; social media applications in learning and research; virtual reality, artificial intelligence, and 3-D modeling applications; the curation of nominal and visual data; and experiential learning spaces, prototyping, gaming, and the Internet of Things. The shift to digital and the implications of scale-based functional work have disrupted broad swaths of the economy, including higher education as service. They are impacting health sciences education, research, clinical care, and community engagement, and are leading to a critical point of inflection for libraries that serve these key mission areas. To embrace the promise of what digitization affords, organizations must shift to thinking (and operating) at scale.

With this in mind, in order to "work at the speed of scale," what must we consider from a *staff readiness* perspective, where expectations around outcomes and performance of work are tied to coordination, alignment, and service delivery in a broad library ecosystem? The authors posit that in health sciences education, both in the academy and in our libraries, scale begs a systems

Gerald Perry and Michael Brewer

approach. This has been recognized in the health-care delivery environment, evinced by the emergence of large, often multistate care-delivery networks.[5] In the academy, libraries have historically operated at scale by leveraging resource-sharing consortia, collaborative preservation networks, and purchasing cooperatives.[6] Increasingly, scale is also a factor at the local level, where universities and university systems now expect their libraries to find ways to bring the advantages of scale to bear. Whether those advantages end up being manifest in the form of enhanced or expanded client services and/or in significant cost savings or efficiencies, they are generally brought about not only through leveraging digital technology, but also through the thoughtful consolidation, organizational redesign, or merger of service units, including the integration of health sciences or other specialized libraries within general academic libraries.[7] Thinking at scale for organizations typically leads to the merger of services, the combining of functional and transactional work across formerly disparate units, integration of systems, and the colocation of expertise, all resulting in the dissolution of silos and the creation of new, often more complex relationships and codependencies.

Mergers, Integrations, and Assimilations—the Literature

Prior to the "web era," libraries were organized around print.[8] Since the 1990s, librarians' focus has shifted to digital, and many would argue that health sciences libraries were in the vanguard of this transformational realignment; the University of Colorado's Health Sciences Library moved, per policy, to all digital for receipt of its serials as early as 2005.[9] Twelve years hence, such a transition can be seen historically as optimal, even privileged, given the narrower focus of health sciences libraries and the abetting nature of the professions served, where the embrace of digital has largely been informed by the nature of clinical and research commitments. Such incumbencies prioritize disintermediated workflows, allowing practitioners to remain in the clinic or lab, accessing the knowledge base from network-enabled mobile devices. However, even the most progressive of health sciences libraries are not immune to the broader economic, cultural, and political pressures that are driving the embrace of scaled solutions. At the institutional level within higher education, a response to the problems—and opportunities—of scale have, in a number of high-profile cases, been addressed through consolidations and integrations. Mergers of health sciences with general academic libraries pose their own set of unique challenges, not the least of which relate to the provisioning of services to disparate clientele (often with unique needs or expectations), all in a context often characterized by a clash of cultures. Colleen M. Kenefick and Susan E. Werner's 2013 article describing the merger of Stony Brook University's Health Sciences with

University Libraries succinctly sums up the drivers leading to the consolidation of libraries for that campus:

> For more than 40 years, the Health Sciences Library and the University Libraries had been administered separately with different directors, budgets, staff, and organizational cultures. In 2010, the decision was made to merge these two libraries for reasons currently common to many large research university libraries, including administrative efficiencies and cost savings.[10]

The merger of a health sciences library with a largely undergraduate library that occurred subsequent to the consolidation of two American universities is described by Jeffrey J. Heck et al. in a 2013 *Library Leadership and Management* article. In this article, the authors note that

> [c]onsolidation serves as one tool available to statewide educational regulatory groups such as a board of regents, who seek cost saving measures in higher education. Two Georgia universities recently completed a consolidation, finding a natural fit of combining a professional health-sciences university with a largely undergraduate liberal arts university. While there were obstacles to completing the consolidation, including the cultures of the universities, the consolidation has been completed and development toward a comprehensive high-level research university has begun. The consolidation was cooperative, and it involved joining two libraries with different foci in the span of one year.[11]

Summarizing their findings about library consolidations, Heck et al. noted that "[o]verall, lessons learned from academic library consolidation as reported in the literature focused on the importance of providing sustained and positive leadership; maximizing staff participation and buy-in, planning all aspects of the consolidation effort; and effective and timely communication among all participants."

Leadership, participation, and communication were critical elements of the integration of the University of Arizona Health Sciences Library (UAHSL) within the UAL system at the University of Arizona, a process that was launched in 2013 with the hiring of a new dean for the UAL. The UAHSL, then known as the Arizona Health Sciences Library, had experienced a number of consecutive years of constraint subsequent to budget cuts. Upon the new dean's arrival, it was determined that a change of report for the UAHSL to the UAL system was an optimal, scale-informed solution for addressing these and other challenges faced by the UAHSL, including its ability to provide a full complement of services to its clients and deliver on its mission to the health sciences campus. Leveraging scale as afforded by integration was thusly embraced, though some integration had already occurred on a small, tacit scale with the coordination of interlibrary lending and document-provisioning services and the consolidation of the two libraries' integrated library systems.

Where it made best sense in terms of work flow efficiencies and economies of scale, functional work units were merged organically over time between 2014 and 2016 after an initial series of trust-building efforts, which included UAHSL all-staff meetings with the dean and the integration of UAHSL's director onto UAL's cabinet leadership team. Once the context and framework for consolidation were articulated, the libraries' leadership advanced with the integration, eventually leading to the centralization or locus of support for acquisitions, resource sharing, collections, business office/human resources, facilities, and administrative staff at the UAL Main Library. Frontline client reference, directional, and facilities-related transactional services were coordinated by the creation of a single team for staffing and supporting all UAL system service points from a single department led out of the Main Library, with dedicated cohorts of staff distributed among service sites. Liaison librarians remained embedded in the colleges they served on the health sciences campus in recognition of a very successful embedded service model deployed in 2007 and deeply embraced by these academic units ever since.[12]

Writing about the Georgia universities' consolidation, Heck et al. noted that

> [t]he successful transition of personnel into the new university is the most difficult goal for any consolidation. Cultural values can be a particular source of conflict if balanced representation from both locations is not present during the strategic planning process. It is critical to provide constant communication of changes and to demonstrate the advantages of consolidation.[13]

In the case of UAHSL's merger within the UAL system, communications were managed by the new UAL dean and the director of the UAHSL, and coordination around planning was executed through the UAL's cabinet. In 2015, the UAHSL director retired and a new associate dean for health sciences and strategic planning and director of UAHSL (author Gerald Perry) was recruited. The new associate dean/director's portfolio was intentionally expanded to include oversight of the research and learning units from both the Main and Health Sciences libraries in recognition of his reference, research, and education-oriented professional experience and background. This change in reporting relationships not only introduced the potential to provide more cohesive liaison services across the libraries and provide them at scale (with all liaisons reporting up through a single associate dean), it also created a venue for the two distinct organizational cultures to begin to acculturate to one another.

Case Study: The University of Arizona Libraries Research and Learning

At the UAL, including the UAHSL, the research and learning librarians function as liaisons to specific colleges and the academic departments and programs within them, providing services directly, when possible, and acting as concierges for specialized or emerging service needs. This model of service is predicated on the challenge of serving large numbers of faculty and students, all with diverse needs and in an environment of rapid change, at scale. The approach takes into consideration the local programmatic needs of the campuses served while respecting their cultural differences as well as those of the recently merged libraries.

Strategically preparing for the scaled delivery of existing and emerging research and learning services utilizing a liaison model, and the administrative readiness efforts to position liaison and specialist librarians for success, serves as a case study in the reinvention of this critical librarian role and is the subject of the remainder of this chapter.

Liaisons and Specialists: A Hybrid Model

The UAL's approach to the work of liaisons is informed by the 2013 Association of Research Libraries' (ARL) *New Roles for New Times: Transforming Liaison Roles in Research Libraries*, authored by Janice Jaguszewski and Karen Williams, who at the time of its writing were colleagues at the University of Minnesota.[14] Williams is now dean of libraries and interim vice president for information technology and chief information officer at the University of Arizona. In summarizing the current challenge for academic liaison librarians, Jaguszewski and Williams note,

> While there is general agreement that liaison roles are changing, research librarians are grappling with the scope of these new roles. Identifying emerging roles, determining what work to divest of, designing supportive institutional structures, establishing areas of primacy and leadership on campus and ensuring that liaisons have needed skills and knowledge all present collective and urgent challenges.[15]

In preparing their ARL publication, Jaguszewski and Williams interviewed administrative teams at five ARL libraries and discerned "a trend toward a hybrid model, where liaisons pair their expertise with that of functional specialists, both within and outside of libraries."[16] Thusly, the hybrid model for delivery of research and learning services has emerged in the UAL system, and our approach to librarian readiness has been informed by a number of the salient features of the trend that Jaguszewski and Williams identified in their research:

Gerald Perry and Michael Brewer

Unpacking this trend a bit reveals a variety of factors at play, and many libraries are employing a systems view of workforce development that considered multiple elements. . . . Blurring of librarian and support staff roles, a wave of retirements, difficulties in hiring and retaining technical staff, and a desire for libraries' staff makeup to better reflect the diversity represented by their clientele are all challenges that libraries face.[17]

Our approach is also rooted in the idea of "deep or radical collaboration" as posited by Jaguszewski and Williams, where staff routinely work "across traditional silos such as department and divisional boundaries, across campus where we need to partner with faculty and other professionals and across institutional boundaries, meeting a dramatic need for libraries to work together."[18] While teams of research and learning librarians at both the UAHSL and the UAL had been active in rethinking their models of service, librarian roles, and the optimal organizational structures to support them in the years prior to the consolidation,[19] the expanded context and significant opportunity born of the merger compelled us as a new entity to collectively revisit the assumptions that had guided our service models and past practice as independent libraries.

As previously noted, since 2007 the UAHSL had been deploying an embedded model of liaison librarianship. In their 2016 *Medical Reference Services Quarterly* article "An Embedded Librarian Program: Eight Years On," authors Gary Freiburger, Jennifer M. Martin, and Annabelle Nuñez reflect on the UAHSL experience with an embedded liaison librarianship model, echoing Jaguszewski and Williams and their call for radical collaboration. According to the authors, "Strong relationships have been built between librarians, faculty members, and students. Locating the librarians among faculty and students led to a better understanding of client needs and an increased awareness of librarian competencies and services resulting in partnerships and greater utilization of library services."[20]

Their success is paralleled by successes achieved at the Main Library of the UAL system, where the subject specialist model had been abandoned some years earlier in favor of what evolved into a more scaled "college coordinator" model. This model put a greater emphasis on conducting intentional, iterative needs assessment and on scaling our services at the college and program levels. While it would be premature to call this a hybrid liaison model, it was certainly a step in that direction, with its explicit focus on needs assessment and in its recognition of the need to operate at greater scale than the subject specialist model had previously afforded. The UAL had also developed a unit of librarians with specialist roles in support of our digital library and the emerging digital needs of researchers and scholars. The Office of Digital Innovation and Stewardship, as it is presently called, provides a broad range of services and expertise to support digital scholarship and stewardship within the broader context of the university's and libraries' strategic plans. These services and expertise include oversight of library services related to metadata, our campus repository, local digital collections, journal hosting, data management, geospatial data, copyright, and scholarly communication, including open access initiatives. Individuals from this unit now work in "radical collaboration" with liaison librarians, both at the Main and Health Sciences libraries to support these and other specialized client needs across campus. It is critical at this juncture to note that these specialist-supported services represent a significant addition to the resources and services available to health sciences constituencies as a benefit of the libraries' consolidation.

In many ways, while the new, unified UAL was already organized and operating using a hybrid liaison–like model shortly after Dean Williams arrived, it was doing so in pockets or at the individual relationship level, not intentionally at a systems level. The different organizational cultures and practices of the merged libraries, as well as the hiring of multiple new liaison librarians and upper administrators (not to mention the lack of agreed upon work flows, assumptions, service levels, or indicators of success related to liaison practice), required that we explicitly describe and operationalize an institutional hybrid liaison services approach to more formally guide our practice. In order to accomplish this, in 2015 the UAL cabinet empaneled an ad hoc Research, Teaching and Learning Task Force co-led by the head responsible for the Research and Learning Department at the Main Library (author Michael Brewer) and the UAHSL associate director for research and learning (the supervisor responsible for the embedded librarian program). Membership in the task force was intentionally broad and included members of the Research and Learning Department at the Main Library, embedded librarians from the UAHSL, an archivist from UAL Special Collections, and a senior librarian operating in a specialist role from the ODIS.

The charge extended to this ad hoc task force was "to define the UAL's Hybrid Liaison Model for engaging academic units, including core and specialized services and knowledge." Over a period of several months in 2015, the task force consulted the literature on liaison librarianship, met with and interviewed UAL librarians in liaison roles, including the embedded librarians at the UAHSL, and prepared a document outlining recommendations for operationalizing the hybrid model throughout the UAL system. Central to the work of the task force were: defining roles of personnel within the model's framework; articulating the individualized roles and responsibilities of liaisons/embedded librarians; describing the roles and responsibilities of specialists working within the UAL system; describing the requirements and expectations for effective referrals/

handoffs between personnel in the performance of their roles, with a focus on communications between liaisons and specialists; and suggesting new areas of engagement for liaison and specialists. The document was presented to UAL departments for comment, revised iterations were subsequently shared across the UAL system, and a final version was presented to and affirmed by the cabinet in 2016.

Readiness for New Roles

As the old adage goes, hindsight is 20/20. Looking at the work of the Research, Teaching and Learning Task Force in late 2016, it is clear to the authors that the document has utility as a kind of "readiness roadmap" for preparing librarians, and the library, for the evolving roles of liaisons in the research library ecology. Seen as such, there are key milestones along the way toward readiness: embracing the hybrid approach, in acknowledgment of the complexity of meeting contemporaneous client needs of the library when operating at scale; articulating shared expectations to which librarians fulfilling liaison and specialist roles must be held accountable in order to execute on the needs of clients; delineating roles and articulating core services provided by liaisons as well as the functions of specialist librarians and staff; articulating a consensus around communications expectations as essential to the conveyance and delivery of services where and when they are needed; asserting individual and institutional responsibilities for training and expert support for the work of liaisons; and recognizing the importance of scalability if success is to be achieved.

According to task force recommendations, "Every liaison does not need to know everything; responsibility for the growth needed to fulfill emerging needs is shared but is guided by real and anticipated client needs. Specialists are responsible for working with liaisons to close gaps between liaisons' current skills or knowledge levels and the 'core' needs and 'baseline' service levels required by their units in specialty areas."[21] The recommendations document goes on to note that "[t]he scalability of the hybrid model rests in the fact that it efficiently uses the skills and knowledge of specialists to provide services across all academic units on campus, unburdening liaisons of the need to be expert in all things. This model can only be scalable, however, if referrals are made to specialists appropriately, lines of communication are open and active, and service data is recorded, well-organized, and broadly available to all staff."[22] These recommendations regarding scale echo learnings previously noted from the literature on consolidations of libraries, wherein frequent, deliberate, and transparent communications about the intention of the integration are critical to insuring success.[23]

The Argument for Scale

It is the authors' view that, ultimately, the ability to meet the emerging needs of our libraries' clients demands solutions at scale. The growing complexity of participating in the research enterprise, the insistence on accountability for outcomes in teaching and learning, the urgent need to expedite the application of new learnings in high-stakes clinical contexts, and the incumbencies on the academy to bring solutions forth for addressing community challenges are all, taken cumulatively, overwhelming and require scalable approaches. Assets within our libraries-as-organizations, and even assets across institutional divisions such as those that separate health sciences from general academic libraries, must be leveraged.

As previously noted, such leveraging does not come without consequences, especially for the staff who are most directly impacted. As shown in the literature on library mergers, and exemplified in the University of Arizona case study, leadership, broad participation, and robust communication are essential to bridging cultural differences that slow progress and limit collaboration. Fundamentally, personnel must be assured of their positions and roles in the organization, and effort must be invested in preparing staff. Systems approaches necessarily entail the careful articulation of responsibilities and the rightsizing of work portfolios such that the efforts of few can be orchestrated to meet the needs of many.

It is also critical to articulate a shared understanding of what success "looks like" to the librarians and staff who are performing in their roles.[24] This is particularly critical when, in a consolidated environment, librarians are serving very diverse sets of clients. The needs of faculty in fine arts are very different from those in medicine. The model of scale thus demands that library leaders work with their librarians to set expectations for liaisons that reasonably account for differences in clientele needs and their willingness to engage with and take advantage of services offered. The inherent elasticity of the hybrid model approach to liaison service delivery (wherein the needs of clients are fulfilled or referred in a triaging system of support, leveraging specialist expertise throughout the library-as-organization) abets the library's response to this cultural variability. It additionally allows for balancing the immediate demands for access by clients to established, day-to-day services with the need on the part of the library to provide capacity for staff to be continually exploring and pursuing new strategic opportunities.

Lessons Learned

One lesson learned through the UAL experience is that liaisons and specialists are more often roles that librarians fill as a portion of their workload than they are cleanly delineated positions at 1.0 FTE. Active liaisons who appropriately pursue opportunities to fulfill emerging client needs will often find themselves, at least temporarily, playing the role of specialist when those same needs begin to emerge across other disciplines (e.g., text mining, data visualization, 3-D scanning and printing, etc.). Likewise, specialists may frequently find themselves serving as connectors to other specialists or to liaisons, especially for clients they work with often. As such, a certain amount of cushion must be built into the system, especially when it comes to determining workloads, assessing performance, and supporting professional development opportunities. Working from core principles, general guidelines, and broad indicators of success were found to be of much greater utility than attempting to more finely tune or fully standardize expectations and practice across the board. Also, because in today's dynamic academic environment, an area of emerging need can quickly balloon into a major service area (e.g., data management planning, responding to campus open access mandates for faculty authored journal articles, Open Educational Resources adoptions, etc.), administrators must carefully monitor needs and ascertain when and how to appropriately increase specialized support, whether that is by moving a liaison who has pioneered early service support in an area into a full-time specialist role, distributing the specialist workload across several liaisons by pruning other duties from their job descriptions, or hiring in or repurposing another position to rightsize support for the burgeoning service area.

Another lesson learned has been the importance of developing and maintaining a current institutional inventory of expertise (in current and emerging functional and service areas, including linguistic and subject knowledge, technical expertise, etc.), not only to facilitate quick and appropriate referrals and support for liaisons, but also to provide other library units (e.g., tech services, resource sharing, collections, development, etc.) with quick and easy access to the rich pool of skills and knowledge resident in the libraries. The effective scaling of institutional skills and expertise that are necessary for a successful hybrid liaison program will fall short of what is possible without the awareness and quick access an inventory of this type can afford.

Lastly, a lesson learned (but not yet fully addressed) has been the need for macro-level monitoring and analysis of patterns and levels of service across the system, including assessing and reporting on the impact, outcomes, and value of the service provided to the programs/units served.[25] What does the overall profile or contour of our service outputs to the campus or to individual programs or colleges (e.g., engineering, nursing, fine arts, etc.) look like? Where are our resources, in services rendered, flowing? Where are we seeing success and where might there be opportunities to fill service gaps? Some libraries see potential in investigating customer management software, such as SalesForce, as a solution for this level of data capture and analysis.[26]

Scale and Its Implications for Health Sciences Libraries

For the academic health sciences library, consolidation or integration with a general academic "sister" library is not without its controversies. It may entail a loss of autonomy in decision making, a perceived slowing in the pace of work, and a sense that one is losing the immediacy of contact with one's primary clientele in order to be a "true citizen" of a larger system. Each individual library context is necessarily specific to a set of local conditions; it is the authors' position, based on their experience at the University of Arizona, that consolidation has brought scale to bear in an effective and meaningful way to the clientele of both the general academic and health sciences campuses. This has opened up opportunities for greater cross-campus collaborations through the coordinating efforts of the libraries and, in the case of the health sciences library, made available a range of services that otherwise might not have been feasible, due largely to the benefits of the scope and depth of programming offered by the university's library system.

For the specialist health sciences library, serving industry or operating in clinical settings, the lessons learned from operating at "the speed of scale" are also applicable. Hospital librarians pivoting to meet the changing needs of their clientele are likely to find themselves functioning as specialists as new roles and identities are delineated. Well-networked hospital librarians will be in as much a need to refer and triage clients, and leverage their networks of colleagues and known experts, as their colleagues in the academy. Lastly, special or clinical librarians will need to develop the necessary assessment metrics for demonstrating the value proposition for maintaining a library—and librarian—and may find the benefits of scale an important option to leverage.

Acknowledgment

The authors wish to acknowledge and thank the members of the University of Arizona Libraries' Research, Teaching, and Learning Task Force:

- Veronica Reyes-Escudero, Special Collections
- Jennifer Nichols, Research and Learning
- Jennifer Martin, University of Arizona Health Sciences Library
- Sandy Kramer, Co-Chair, University of Arizona Health Sciences Library
- Mary Feeney, Research and Learning
- Michael Brewer, Co-Chair, Research and Learning
- Christine Kollen, Office of Digital Innovation and Stewardship

Notes

1. See "The Fourth Industrial Revolution, by Klaus Schwab," World Economic Forum website, accessed August 6, 2017, https://www.weforum.org/about/the-fourth-industrial-revolution-by-klaus-schwab.
2. See "Join the iSpace Community," University of Arizona Libraries website, accessed August 6, 2017, https://new.library.arizona.edu/visit/spaces/ispace and "Borrow Technology," University of Arizona Libraries website, accessed August 6, 2017, https://new.library.arizona.edu/tech/borrow.
3. See *New Ideas Start Here*, University Libraries Strategic Plan, 2015-2018, accessed August 6, 2017, http://www.library.arizona.edu/sites/default/files/UAL_Strategic Plan_2015-18.pdf.
4. Carla J. Stoffle and Cheryl Cuillier, "From Surviving to Thriving," *Journal of Library Administration* 51, no. 1 (2010): 130-55, doi: 10.1080/01930826.2011.531645.
5. Dan Beckham, "Hospitals Choosing to Join Networks Instead of Merging," *Hospital and Health Networks*, April 14, 2014, accessed August 6, 2017, http://www.hhnmag.com/articles/4257-hospitals-choosing-to-join-networks-instead-of-merging.
6. J. J. Koop, "Library Consortia and Information Technology: The Past, the Present, the Promise," *Information Technology and Libraries* 17, no. 1 (1998): 7-12.
7. Jeffrey J. Heck et al., "Consolidation: A Tale of Two Libraries," *Library Leadership and Management*, 28, no. 1 (2013): 1-14.
8. David W. Lewis, "A Strategy for Academic Libraries in the First Quarter of the 21st Century," *College and Research Libraries* 68, no. 5 (2007): 418-34.
9. The UAL also shifted during this same period to a "single format" approach to information resources, where digital, if available, was the preferred format.
10. Colleen M. Kenefick and Susan E. Werner, "Prescription for Reorganizing: Merging Campus Libraries," *Public Services Quarterly* 9, no. 3 (2013): 260.
11. Heck et al., "Consolidation," 1.
12. Gary Freiburger, Jennifer M. Martin, and Annabelle Nuñez, "An Embedded Librarian Program: Eight Years On," *Medical Reference Services Quarterly* 35, no. 4 (2016): 388-96.
13. Heck et al., "Consolidation," 2.
14. Janice M. Jaguszewski and Karen Williams, *New Roles for New Times: Transforming Liaison Roles in Research Libraries* (Washington, DC: Association for Research Libraries, 2013), accessed August 6, 2017, http://www.arl.org/component/content/article/6/2893.
15. Ibid., 4.
16. http://www.arl.org/publications-resources/2893-new-roles-for-new-times-transforming-liaison-roles-in-research-libraries#.WW_ZUIqQzPQ on page 4.
17. Ibid., 14.
18. http://www.arl.org/publications-resources/2893-new-roles-for-new-times-transforming-liaison-roles-in-research-libraries#.WW_ZUIqQzPQ on page 14.
19. See, for example, Freiburger, Martin, and Nuñez, "An Embedded Librarian Program"; M. E. Feeney et al., "*A New Approach to Needs Assessment and Communication to Connect and Collaborate with Faculty*," Special Libraries Association (SLA), June 2013, accessed August 6, 2017, https://www.sla.org/wp-content/uploads/2013/07/Tues-ElliotMartin-NeedsAssessment.pdf; and Ricardo R. Andrade and Raik Zaghloul, "Restructuring

Liaison Librarian Teams at the University of Arizona Libraries, 2007-2009," *New Library World.* 111, no. 7/8 (2010): 273-86. doi: 10.1108/03074801011059911.

20. Freiburger, Martin, and Nuñez, "An Embedded Librarian Program," 388.
21. The task force's early 2016 report, *Research, Teaching, and Learning Task Force Recommendations,* is available from the authors upon request.
22. Ibid.
23. Heck, *"Consolidation."*
24. Robyn Hull-Eibl, Jeanne F. Voyles, and Michael M. Brewer, "Competency-Based Hiring, Job Descriptions, and Performance Goals: The Value of an Integrated System," *Journal of Library Administration.* 51, no. 7-8 (2011): 673-91.
25. While this level of assessment certainly does encompass individual service transactions (reference consultations, instructional sessions, etc.), it is more concerned with larger patterns of use across the institution, with the impact of our services on academic degree programs and overall student success, as well as on research activities, including the stewardship of and broad accessibility to UA-generated research results.
26. The topic of Customer Relation Management systems and their potential for use in this manner has been a topic of conversation at the Association for Research Libraries Library Liaison Meeting, most recently as the American Library Association Annual Conference in June 2016.

Chapter 9

Solo Librarians

Meredith Solomon and Meghan Muir

Change and reorganization in small academic and hospital health sciences libraries is inevitable. This chapter will discuss issues and challenges such as managing work flow and changing roles, solutions such as continuing education and professional development, and how solo and small-staff libraries can empower themselves and their staff to manage reorganization and change and ultimately benefit from it.

The transformation of libraries and library staff is crucial in order to keep pace with the ever-changing health-care environment. Hospital and other small health sciences librarians may be faced with organizational change due to reorganization of the parent institution, and its reduced budget and resources, reduction in library staff, and loss of physical library space. Libraries have the capability to mitigate these changes with strategies, confidence, and bravery. It is imperative that librarians in small health sciences libraries demonstrate that their libraries add value and remain vital to their parent organization.

It is common for librarians at small libraries to be responsible for all library operations. Reference and instruction, collection development, electronic resources, administration, and management are all part of the hospital librarian's job. Librarians who are solely in charge of their hospital libraries or work in small health sciences libraries with four or fewer staff have all probably felt that they are working within a vacuum within their parent organizations. They may also feel isolated from their fellow health sciences librarians. Each day brings new roles and opportunities to librarians staffing a small hospital library. There are increased demands from library users on library staff. The culture of the library is time poor and the pace of its work environment, especially in health care, is ever increasing. In general, the health-care workforce feels as if there is less time to do more work. Managing work flow, time management, and skill building are essential tactics for small library staff.

Solo librarians are faced with a shared dilemma: there just isn't enough time in the day to get it all done! One essential skill is time management. What is the best way to handle the myriad requests for help encountered in one day? A constant onslaught of e-mails, phone calls, chat reference, and in-person questions is the norm. How do solo librarians manage the inundation of new requests while also maintaining library operations? One tactic is to set expectations. While this is not exactly a positive customer service strategy, and may go against the librarian's nature, it may be necessary to learn to say "No" or "Not right now."

When considering skill building and transformation for small library staff, it is important to remember that the needs of library users often dictates which skills should be developed. Working in a small library inherently makes staff more reactive based on the immediate needs of users. Adaptability is one of many skills solo and small-staff librarians must embrace. Downsizing of hospital library staff can be attributed in part to major changes in the health-care environment.[1] Library managers and directors, whether solo or managing a small staff, need to adapt to unstable staffing levels in their own libraries.[2]

Hospital libraries in particular have evolved regularly in an effort to sustain their presence in the institution and to prove their value to administration. A wealth of published studies report the impact of health sciences library services and the effect on patient care and scholarly output of an institution or hospital.[3] Librarians should consider conducting a survey of their own that will proactively provide a standard measure of how library services support their institutions' missions. It is important to track outcomes, such as how the information provided might change practice or avoid an adverse event, using such quantitative measures as statistics.

Solo librarians must also engage in upskilling and updating job competencies. One survey of health sciences librarians in academic and hospital settings sought to examine the reasons driving changes in job duties. As with most libraries, hospital librarians reported that "changes in access and delivery of information" was the most common reason that library job duties changed. Other reasons included "changing needs of users," "budget issues," and "changes in technology."[4] Information professionals working as solo librarians must commit

Meredith Solomon and Meghan Muir

to learning new skills and taking advantage of professional development opportunities. Librarians who manage a small staff must encourage and support their employees to embrace a culture of growth, improvement, and professional development.

One unique aspect of working in a solo or small library is the impact of isolation. Certainly, a solo librarian may feel as if he or she is on an island within the organization, but even those working in small libraries might feel separated from the larger organization for which they work. Feeling like part of a team is an important factor in work-related happiness. One recent meta-analysis on the importance of individuals' social identification within in an organization showed how it affected leadership, motivation, and communication. N. K. Steffens and his team concluded "that social identifications in organizations are just as important for individuals' health and well-being as they are for their productivity and performance."[5]

Disruption to workflow in libraries is old news. Continual changes in technology and shifts in user needs are commonplace in the library environment. Despite this, it is normal for library staff to struggle with changes in existing work flow or to be concerned with possible upcoming work flow disruptions due to reorganization or other institutional changes. Reorganization and change inevitably affect work flow and how librarians do their jobs. Hospital libraries already face challenges with work flow due to reduced staff and resources, physical space changes, hospital system (and library) consolidation or mergers, and staff burnout.

Changes to existing work flow might arise for any number of reasons, and in small libraries any absence will inevitably affect work flow. In environments where librarians feel at capacity, changes to work flow can cause stress and frustration. It is important to know how to handle and better prepare for such changes.

Time management is one of the solo librarian's "greatest tool[s]" in order to "do it all."[6] Being organized and maintaining some type of schedule of tasks first comes to mind when thinking about time management, but one of the many keys to success is flexibility. Solo librarians in hospitals know a well-planned day of budget tasks, for example, will be thrown to the wayside when a library user needs help finding information for patient care. This is a common occurrence. Time management involves not only simple strategic measures such as prioritizing a to-do list and building gaps in the daily schedule to accommodate unexpected interruptions, but also managing the best use of time. Peter Drucker's famous quote "Efficiency is concerned with doing things right[; e]ffectiveness is doing the right things" states this idea perfectly.[7] Doing tasks just because "that is how it has always been done" is not always effective.

Increasingly busy schedules, interruptions, and doing it all alone or with a small staff will ultimately cause librarians to feel overwhelmed, stressed, or burnt out. Managing stress is difficult and often falls to the bottom of the priority list. No matter how small or large the workplace of the twenty-first century is, more focus on wellness for employees, flexible schedules, and work-life balance is necessary. A library with a small staff might have more options for flexible work schedules than a library with a single staff member. Engaging in professional development activities can also relieve stress.[8] Even if in-person attendance at a conference or workshop is not possible, there are many online and free professional development opportunities available from various library organizations. Learning something new or connecting with colleagues and sharing experiences is empowering and can help alleviate isolation, stress, and feeling overwhelmed.

Preparing to do things differently can be stressful. Fearing the unknown is a normal response to change. Unfortunately, there are many stories of libraries large and small downsizing and closing. T. Scott Plutchak eloquently poses a possible approach to change or reorganization that is applicable to any size library:

> Our job is not to build a better library, but to figure out how we can best use our tools and talents to advance the mission of the university. Sometimes that'll mean continuing to do the things that people have always associated with libraries, sometimes it will mean no longer doing some of those things. And sometimes it will mean taking on things that no one ever associated with a library before.[9]

Reorganization may be initiated for a number of reasons, such as reducing inefficient operational practices or reducing budgets. People often panic when faced with such changes, perhaps fearing it will change the way the library operates in a negative way. This is not always the case. When libraries merge or are consolidated, it can allow for more efficient operations, and the economic savings can be used for increased staff or more robust services and resources. Paying attention to staff and personnel issues before, during, and after reorganization is essential. It is important for small-library managers and directors to be transparent and include staff in planning and communication. When staff feel left out, they may also feel powerless and demoralized. Strategies to help manage feelings of powerlessness and avoid demoralization include creating opportunities for staff to voice concerns and ideas, assisting with goal setting to increase their investment in the change process, and providing additional training to help with changing tasks and work flow.[10]

Solo librarians faced with reorganization may not have a librarian supervisor to help coach or advise on the future direction of the library. It is up to the solo librarian to take charge, to identify key library advocates and stakeholders in the organization, and to "pivot" with the parent organizational changes and adjust library services as necessary.[11] Small-staff libraries face similar problems; the library manager or director has the added task of empowering library staff to embrace such change. In both cases, this might require changing daily work flow, learning new skills, embracing more professional development opportunities, and understanding basic change management strategies.

Wayne Finley, business librarian and assistant professor at Northern Illinois University Libraries, employed a personal selling technique to start an embedded librarianship program at his library. According to Finley, "The goal of personal selling is to use interpersonal communication to inform customers about products and services and persuade them to make purchases."[12] In most small or solo hospital libraries, patrons are not necessarily purchasing products or services, although there are sometimes fees for some services or cost sharing for resources. However, "making purchases" in this context might be seen as the act of using library resources or engaging with library staff for services. Finley explains further: "If a reference librarian saw a patron struggling to find information and wandering aimlessly through the stacks, and then convinced that patron to use specific library resources to meet that information need, the librarian is in effect engaging in personal selling."[13]

Librarians cannot be all things to all people, but focus should be on reaching library patrons (both current users and nonusers) where an impact can be made. Since not all hospital employees will need to use the library, it may be worthwhile to focus outreach efforts on finding the potential users who might benefit most from its services. Library administrators should investigate user groups within the institution who need library services and approach them with ideas about how the library can help their mission, whether it is simply introducing them to online resources or offering a brief instruction session at department meetings.

Library administrators should also go beyond the reactive way of working, proactively seeking out users' needs. They should consider not only current library users, who know what library services are available, but also nonusers, showing them how a librarian's expertise will add value to their work. Pivoting to meet the needs of users and respond to unstable environments is essential.[14] Fostering new collaborations to help others reach their goals—whether related to research, patient care, continuing education, or day-to-day functions of their jobs—is how library staff can help. Library administrators should elevate themselves to the position of expert and be confident in explaining their knowledge and skills to others in order to help them do a better job.

What do continuing education, professional development, and lifelong learning mean to a solo or small-staff medical library? Librarians in these environments are the sole information providers in their institutions; therefore, professional development is essential. No explicit definition of professional development has been given in the literature, but there are myriad ways librarians can gain the knowledge and information needed to help their patrons. E. Hornung detected five categories of continuing professional development in her study: it is for the sake of the organization or library service; it is about development as a professional librarian; it is helping solo librarians accomplish all the tasks they are responsible for; it is when librarians have learned something and want to do things in a better way; and it is about librarians' development as human beings.[15] Hornung's first category—continuing professional development for the sake of the organization/library service—is discussed in more detail in chapter 3. The remaining four categories are ways to describe the numerous methods of acquiring the education needed to serve users.

No matter their size, libraries actively encourage "engagement in activities that enhance and deepen their knowledge."[16] With the digital age upon us and new methods of learning such as virtual reality and smart devices, staying up to date on such technologies and how users access information with them is crucial. However, solo librarians or small-staff libraries may find it difficult to attend courses, meetings, and other forms of professional development due to staffing, scheduling, and workload issues. Availability is not the issue; accessibility is. In order to attend off-site programs, library staff may have to close the library or use paraprofessionals or volunteers while they are away. Librarians in these settings have not only the right but the obligation to themselves, their institutions, and their users to stay current in order to give the best support possible.

Differing perceptions or interpretations of what continuing education looks like is another dilemma held by solo and small-staff libraries. Continuing education can be defined as

> a realization, a commitment, a plan, an activity, and a process . . . [it can also be a] dichotomy between perspectives of the individual and those of the employer with regard to responsibility for continuing professional development and the benefits of this activity.[17]

Those reporting to nonlibrarians and explaining the workload to nonlibrarian managers may find it is difficult for them to understand the support library staff need.[18] For example, a solo librarian may report to the chief medical officer of an organization, a physician responsible for supporting the library but who has very little knowledge about how a library is run and the important skills and education required to be a librarian. Explaining the educational needs of the librarian to such a supervisor is difficult, and the result may be minimal support—in terms of both funding and time—to stay current. Another dilemma in

Meredith Solomon and Meghan Muir

this environment is motivation. What motivates librarians to seek out professional development? There are various motivational factors that can influence a librarian's choice to obtain professional development, including managerial and/or institutional support, personal satisfaction, and self-motivation to become better at something or to learn a new skill.

Where can librarians find professional development courses, training, and workshops? As lifelong learners, librarians are accustomed in seeking opportunities from their peers as well as from related organizations. The following suggestions are relevant not only for solo and small-staff libraries but for any information professional looking to improve upon his or her skills or to learn something new. State, regional, and national organizations offer numerous and various types of professional development in a number of formats. They do not require membership but often reduce fees for members. Another way librarians can engage in professional development is by taking courses at academic institutions as non-degree-seeking students; some colleges and universities offer distance-learning courses or asynchronous courses or have extension offices/centers where students can take courses relevant to individual needs. Platforms such as Massive Open Online Courses or Coursera can also be useful. Internal departments at home institutions, such as the IT department, may offer classes on computer programs the institution supports. Librarians should take advantage of these free opportunities to learn something new as well as to network with employees within the institution.

An additional, more informal opportunity for professional development and continuing education is networking. Many solo and small-staff libraries could not serve their patrons without the resources of the larger library community. This can be done via library organizations, as mentioned earlier in this chapter, as well as through LISTSERVs, informal discussion groups, profession-related meet-ups, and mentoring. "The most important thing for helping us do our jobs better is networking, networking, networking."[19] Keeping in touch with others in the field or finding peers and colleagues outside the parent organization can ameliorate feelings of loneliness or isolation. Networking is all about learning by connecting with people and can offer opportunities for professional development and growth.[20] The main thing for solo librarians to remember is to be creative and find ways to maintain professional connections with other librarians, even those outside the immediate workplace.[21]

Library staff have always adjusted to changing demands, whether from library users or from administrators within the parent organization. As previously discussed, solo and small-staff libraries have historically implemented flexible job descriptions and job duties. Part of managing change, either within a small library or those initiated by an institution, is flexibility.[22]

Remaining relevant and integral to the mission and goals of the parent organization is crucial for the success and longevity of a small health sciences library and cannot be ignored.[23] Understanding how the library fits into the organizational culture is important, but reasons for nonuse of the library should also be explored.

Change does not need to be large or monumental. It is not necessary to stop tasks that are working just for the sake of change. Small, incremental change can be as effective as large change, and may seem more achievable in a small library environment. No matter how or when change occurs, small health science libraries have little to no buffer and are affected quickly.

One common reason a library experiences organizational change/reorganization is loss of space.[24] Solo or small-staff libraries may not occupy large spaces to begin with, but it is all prime real estate in a hospital environment. Other circumstances for an organizational change include reorganization of library operations and/or staff. Providence Health Systems in Portland, Oregon, reported on its reorganization and regionalization of library services. A strategic plan was developed for the library, with priorities that were closely in line with the current institutional strategic plan.[25] Reflecting the parent organization's mission and goals can be an important factor in getting buy-in for the library's proposed changes. Another reason for organizational change is the economic challenges health care is facing.[26]

The results of major organizational change can be positive for solo or small libraries. The Providence Health System libraries had operated as four separate libraries, with four small-staff members. The regionalization allowed the four libraries to work in concert with each other, not only to regionalize electronic resources but to also allow staff to work as a team. In this case, there were multiple benefits of the team approach. It allowed for "efficiency and productivity, created less isolation for the staff working alone at smaller sites, increased opportunity for learning from each other, and encouraged collaborative process improvement."[27]

This case provides a small sampling of how solo or small-staff libraries are affected by organizational change. Another recommendation regarding organizational change for solo librarians or leaders of small libraries is open communication with the librarian's manager or supervisor. Open communication will allow the library to stay ahead of impending changes and will make adapting to them easier. Gradual steps toward change make it easier to digest, and users are not impacted as severely. Change is inevitable; therefore, librarians should set an example and take as much of a leadership role in the changing of their organizations as possible.[28]

Meredith Solomon and Meghan Muir

To summarize, increased demand from library users in the health sciences environment forces solo librarians or staff in small libraries to transform in order to remain relevant. Critical issues for solo or small-staff libraries are time management, work flow management, skill building, professional development, and adapting to organizational changes. Present and future leaders need to be aware of such concerns in order to be of value and to be seen as an effective leader within the larger community.

What does the future hold? Asking this question is crucial to remaining flexible as the parent organization changes and library services change as necessary. As professional roles change, job duties and descriptions may not reflect what has traditionally been done. Librarians are lifelong learners, and taking advantage of professional development opportunities is one of many methods to use to transform staff, small or otherwise. Learning new skills allows librarians to leverage competencies in the work environment as well as to feel empowered to participate in the present and the future of their parent institutions.

Notes

1. M. M. Bandy, "Pivoting: Leveraging Opportunities in a Turbulent Health Care Environment," *Journal of the Medical Library Association* 103, no. 1 (2015): 3–13.
2. P. L. Thibodeau and C. J. Funk, "Trends in Hospital Librarianship and Hospital Library Services: 1989 to 2006," *Journal of the Medical Library Association* 97, no. 4 (2009): 273–79.
3. K. Dunn et al., "Measuring the Value and Impact of Health Sciences Libraries: Planning an Update and Replication of the Rochester Study," *Journal of the Medical Library Association* 97, no. 4 (October 2009): 308–12; J. G. Marshall, "Measuring the Value and Impact of Health Library and Information Services: Past Reflections, Future Possibilities," *Health Information and Libraries Journal* 24 Suppl 1 (December 2007): 4–17; J. G. Marshall et al., "The Value of Library and Information Services in Patient Care: Results of a Multisite Study," *Journal of the Medical Library Association* 101, no. 1 (2013): 38–46.
4. K. D. McMullen and F. Yeh, "Adapting to Change: A Survey of Evolving Job Descriptions in Medical Librarianship," *Journal of Hospital Librarianship* 13, no. 3 (2013), 249.
5. N. K. Steffens et al., "A Meta-Analytic Review of Social Identification and Health in Organizational Contexts," *Personality and Social Psychology Review* (July 7, 2016), 26.
6. L. Zamora, "The Evolving Role of the Solo Librarian: How to Do It All without Losing Your Mind," *The One-Person Library* 25, no. 5 (2008), 3.
7. P. F. Drucker, *The Effective Executive* (New York: Collins, 2006).
8. L. Cooperman, *Managing the One-Person Library*. Chandos Information Professional Series; Waltham, MA: Elsevier Chandos Publishing, 2015.
9. T. S. Plutchak, "A Librarian out of the Library," *Journal of eScience Librarianship* 5, no. 1 (2016), ell06.3.
10. C. Kenefick and J. A. DeVito, "Five Realities of Hospital Library Mergers," *Journal of Hospital Librarianship* 15, no. 3 (2015): 334–40.

11. Bandy, "Pivoting."
12. W. E. Finley, "Using Personal Selling Techniques in Embedded Librarianship," *Journal of Business & Finance Librarianship* 18, no. 4 (2013): 281.
13. Ibid.
14. Bandy, "Pivoting."
15. E. Hornung, "On Your Own but Not Alone: One-Person Librarians in Ireland and Their Perceptions of Continuing Professional Development," *Library Trends* 61, no. 3 (2013): 675–702.
16. Ibid., 675.
17. J. Broady-Preston. "Continuing Professional Development – Its Role in the Changing Educational and Qualification Landscape of the Information Profession; a Case Study of the U.K. "
18. J. A. Siess, "Flying Solo: Librarian, Manage Thyself," *American Libraries* 30, no. 2 (1999): 32–34.
19. M. Solomon, "Network, Network, Network," *MLA News*, no. 398 (2007): 17.
20. Siess, "Flying Solo."
21. Cooperman, *Managing the One-Person Library*.
22. Ibid.
23. Ibid.
24. G. L. Persily and K. A. Butter, "Reinvisioning and Redesigning 'a Library for the Fifteenth through Twenty-First Centuries': A Case Study on Loss of Space from the Library and Center for Knowledge Management, University of California, San Francisco," *Journal of the Medical Library Association* 98, no. 1 (2010): 44–48; V. A. Lynn, M. FitzSimmons, and C. K. Robinson, "Special Report: Symposium on Transformational Change in Health Sciences Libraries: Space, Collections, and Roles," *Journal of the Medical Library Association* 99, no. 1 (2011): 82–87.
25. H. J. Martin and B. Delawska-Elliott, "Combining Resources, Combining Forces: Regionalizing Hospital Library Services in a Large Statewide Health System," *Journal of the Medical Library Association* 103, no. 1 (2015): 44–48.
26. B. Beals, "Valuing Hospital Library Services: One Small Step for a Solo," *Journal of Hospital Librarianship* 9, no. 3 (2009): 331–34.
27. Martin and Delawska-Elliott, "Combining Resources, Combining Forces," 45.
28. Cooperman, *Managing the One-Person Library*.

References

Bandy, M. M. "Pivoting: Leveraging Opportunities in a Turbulent Health Care Environment." *Journal of the Medical Library Association* 103, no. 1 (January 2015): 3–13.

Beals, B. "Valuing Hospital Library Services: One Small Step for a Solo." *Journal of Hospital Librarianship* 9, no. 3 (2009): 331–34.

Cooperman, L. *Managing the One-Person Library*. Chandos Information Professional Series. Waltham, MA: Elsevier Chandos Publishing, 2015.

Drucker, P. F. *The Effective Executive* [in English]. New York: Collins, 2006.

Dunn, K., K. Brewer, J. G. Marshall, and J. Sollenberger. "Measuring the Value and Impact of Health Sciences Libraries: Planning an Update and Replication of the Rochester Study." *Journal of the Medical Library Association* 97, no. 4 (October 2009): 308–12.

Finley, W. E. "Using Personal Selling Techniques in Embedded Librarianship." *Journal of Business & Finance Librarianship* 18, no. 4 (2013): 279–92.

Hornung, E. "On Your Own but Not Alone: One-Person Librarians in Ireland and Their Perceptions of Continuing Professional Development." *Library Trends* 61, no. 3 (winter 2013): 675–702.

Kenefick, C., and J. A. DeVito. "Five Realities of Hospital Library Mergers." *Journal of Hospital Librarianship* 15, no. 3 (2015): 334–40.

Lynn, V. A., M. FitzSimmons, and C. K. Robinson. "Special Report: Symposium on Transformational Change in Health Sciences Libraries: Space, Collections, and Roles" [in English]. *Journal of the Medical Library Association* 99, no. 1 (January 2011): 82–87.

Marshall, J. G. "Measuring the Value and Impact of Health Library and Information Services: Past Reflections, Future Possibilities." *Health Information and Libraries Journal* 24 Suppl 1 (December 2007): 4–17.

Marshall, J. G., J. Sollenberger, S. Easterby-Gannett, L. K. Morgan, M. L. Klem, S. K. Cavanaugh, K. B. Oliver, et al. "The Value of Library and Information Services in Patient Care: Results of a Multisite Study." *Journal of the Medical Library Association* 101, no. 1 (January 2013): 38–46.

Martin, H. J., and B. Delawska-Elliott. "Combining Resources, Combining Forces: Regionalizing Hospital Library Services in a Large Statewide Health System." *Journal of the Medical Library Association* 103, no. 1 (January 2015): 44–48.

McMullen, K. D., and F. Yeh. "Adapting to Change: A Survey of Evolving Job Descriptions in Medical Librarianship." *Journal of Hospital Librarianship* 13, no. 3 (2013): 246–57.

Persily, G. L., and K. A. Butter. "Reinvisioning and Redesigning 'a Library for the Fifteenth through Twenty-First Centuries': A Case Study on Loss of Space from the Library and Center for Knowledge Management, University of California, San Francisco" [in English]. *Journal of the Medical Library Association: JMLA* 98, no. 1 (January 2010): 44–48.

Plutchak, T. S. "A Librarian out of the Library." *Journal of eScience Librarianship* 5, no. 1 (2016): 7.

Siess, J. A. "Flying Solo: Librarian, Manage Thyself." *American Libraries* 30, no. 2 (1999): 32–34.

Solomon, M. "Network, Network, Network." *MLA News*, no. 398 (2007): 17.

Steffens, N. K., S. A. Haslam, S. C. Schuh, J. Jetten, and R. van Dick. "A Meta-Analytic Review of Social Identification and Health in Organizational Contexts." *Personality and Social Psychology Review* (July 7, 2016).

Thibodeau, P. L., and C. J. Funk. "Trends in Hospital Librarianship and Hospital Library Services: 1989 to 2006" [in English]. *Journal of the Medical Library Association* 97, no. 4 (October 2009): 273–79.

Zamora, L. "The Evolving Role of the Solo Librarian: How to Do It All without Losing Your Mind." *One-Person Library* 25, no. 5 (2008): 3.

Chapter 10

Staff Recruitment, Retention, and Reward

Shannon D. Jones

In 2004, Donald Rumsfeld said, "You go to war with the army you have, not the army you might want or wish to have at a later time." This quote sums up my perspective on staff recruitment, retention, and reward. While the war analogy is a little far-fetched in relation to the work of the library, the underlying meaning behind the statement is applicable. The reality that Rumsfeld faced with the United States Army is the same that a new library director or manager faces. We need to work with the personnel already in place. However competent the inherited staff may be, a new manager may find that while some staff embrace change, others will not, and some won't have the skills required to help the library grow to its full potential. Regardless of staff members' attitudes or skills, it is the manager's job to help them reach their greatest potential as employees—ensuring the library's most important resource can tackle the challenges faced in the twenty-first century.

How can a manager identify and fill gaps in staffing? How can a manager recruit and retain high-performing employees who can form a diverse and vibrant library staff? How does a manager reward staff members who go above and beyond in helping the library meet the needs of its parent organization? The answers to these questions will be explored in this chapter.

Identifying Gaps

Merriam-Webster defines a *gap* as "an incomplete or deficient area."[1] Today's libraries are very different from our parents' libraries. Librarians are taking on new roles that require new knowledge and skill sets. A key aspect of these new roles is assessing the strengths and weaknesses of existing staff and measuring them against the library's strategic goals and priorities, which should align with the parent organization's goals. This will allow the library to identify any gaps that need to be filled. One important factor to be aware of is new campus or library initiatives that may require additional staff. Administrators should have an ear on the street and be prepared to deal with any emerging priorities.

With regard to current staffing, strength-and-weakness assessments can help identify gaps in knowledge and identify areas for improvement. This can also be done for the library as a whole. A strategy that the Medical University of South Carolina (MUSC) Libraries used when developing its current strategic plan was to have the library's personnel complete the appreciative inquiry process. D. L. Cooperrider defines appreciative inquiry (AI) as "the cooperative, co-evolutionary search for the best in people, their organizations, and the world around them. It involves systematic discovery of what gives life to an organization or a community when it is most effective and most capable in economic, ecological, and human terms."[2]

Too often, organizations make decisions without inviting all stakeholders into the discussion. AI is a system intervention strategy that solicits feedback from all staffing levels. AI assumes every organization and community has many untapped resources—what people talk about as past, present, and future capacities, or the positive core. AI links the knowledge and energy of this core directly to an organization or a community's agenda, and changes never thought possible before can be realized.[3] The strategy works best with forward-thinking individuals who are willing to embrace change. By working through AI's 4-D cycle—*discover, dream, design,* and *destiny*—the MUSC Libraries personnel were able to create a shared vision for the library's future.

AI is a narrative-based process of positive change. It is a cycle of activity that starts by engaging all members of an organization or community in a broad set of interviews and deep dialogue about strengths, resources, and capabilities.[4] Beginning with the discovery phase, the group is encouraged to think about what in the organization's environment gives it life. During this phase, the group is asked to articulate the organization's strengths and best practices. The group is then asked to dream about what the organization might become in order to create a clear, results-oriented vision. The question posed during this phase is: What is the world calling us to become? During the third phase, the group is encouraged to design what that vision should look like. In the fourth and final phase, the group is expected to create the vision that will lead to an organization's destiny. The AI process is empowering and puts ownership in the hands of the library's personnel. The main benefit of using this process is that it

Shannon D. Jones

offered MUSC Library staff members an opportunity to think about the things they appreciated most about their library and, more importantly, allowed them to be active participants in creating the library's new vision statement.

Know Thyself

Recruitment and retention efforts are very personal activities, and as a manager, an important factor to consider is your own personality. Joel Peterson— lecturer at Stanford Graduate School of Business and chairman of JetBlue Airways—likens an organization's personnel to an investment. He writes, "Like a good investment, finding a great person takes diligence, care and often time. It means locating the best candidates, interviewing them carefully, doing in-depth reference checking, and coaching them well once they're on board."[5] Peterson notes that the most common mistake hiring managers make is repeatedly hiring employees just like themselves. He cautions managers from falling into the trap of selecting candidates who look and act like they do. Similarities in experience, attitude, political views, and physical appearance all increase the likelihood that people will connect—even if those similarities are hiding weaknesses that make the person ill suited for the job.[6] Administrators should keep the library's vision at the forefront of all recruitment, retention, and staff development decisions.

Hiring managers must remain aware that unconscious biases are at play in our lives every day. Even the decisions and actions of the most well-intentioned people are impacted by unconscious bias. J. Moule writes that unconscious biases affect all of our relationships, whether they are fleeting or longer term.[7] The same dynamic undoubtedly holds true in the libraries. Eric Kofee Acree et al. note that "supervisors also need to examine their own personal values and racial biases. This would include not only personal issues around racism, but institutional racism as well."[8] From this perspective, it is impossible for library personnel to participate in recruitment, retention, and development activities without thinking honestly about their own biases, including unconscious ones.

Unconscious biases are more prevalent than conscious biases. Dr. Renee Navarro, vice chancellor for diversity and outreach at the University of Southern California, describes these biases as the attitudes or stereotypes that affect our understanding, actions, and decisions in an unconscious manner: "It is important to note, that biases, conscious or unconscious, are not limited to ethnicity and race. Though racial bias and discrimination is well documented, biases may exist toward any social group. One's age, gender, gender identity physical abilities, religion, sexual orientation, weight, and many other characteristics are subject to bias."[9]Moule notes that unconscious biases lead to unintentional racism—racism that is usually invisible, especially to those who perpetrate it.[10] For example, Moule writes that unconscious bias allows people who consciously desire qualified minority employees to unconsciously rate résumés with black-sounding names as less qualified.[11]

Unconscious bias is likely a contributing factor toward the lack of workforce diversity in a number of institutions, including libraries. One entity that has struggled with a lack of diversity in its higher-level positions is the National Football League (NFL)—a long-standing issue subject to much criticism. On any given Sunday, diversity is apparent on the football field, but that same diversity does not exist in senior-level positions. Like the NFL, libraries historically have notable gaps in the racial and ethnic makeup between lower-level and upper-level positions. It is common to find significant racial diversity among the paraprofessional staff in libraries, but not in managerial positions. In the case of the NFL, B. W. Collins suggests that unconscious bias is to blame for the lack of diversity. In 2002, the NFL implemented a policy known as the Rooney Rule, mandating that every NFL team interview at least one minority candidate upon the vacancy of a head coaching position or be subject to a significant monetary fine.[12] This policy was necessary because the NFL's long-standing hiring practices and networking system consistently allowed front-office decision makers to avoid interacting with qualified African American candidates.[13] At the bare minimum, the Rooney Rule forces decision makers to come face-to-face with candidates they previously may have shunned. While not a perfect cure, recent statistics suggest that the Rooney Rule has succeeded in diversifying the NFL's head-coaching ranks.[14] While libraries cannot take such a punitive approach, one must wonder if the racial and ethnic makeup of library personnel would look different if libraries had a similar rule. Would libraries become more diverse workplaces if managers were aware of unconscious biases and the role they play in keeping qualified minority candidates from having the opportunity to compete for positions? Just like the NFL, library administrators want the best of the best on their team. Recruiting and retaining staff of the highest caliber requires administrators who are self-aware, open-minded leaders who advocate for an inclusive and unbiased hiring process.

Whether hiring or managing staff, administrators and hiring managers can uncover unconscious biases. The first and most important step is admitting that we all have them. Mahzarin R. Banaji et al. write, "Most of us believe that we are ethical and unbiased. We imagine we're good decision makers, able to objectively size up a job candidate or a venture deal and reach a fair and rational conclusion that's in our, and our organization's best interests. But more than two decades of research confirms that, in reality, most of us fall woefully short of our inflated self-perception."[15] Moule adds that people are more likely to act out of unconscious or hidden bias. Knowing you have a bias for or against a particular group may cause you to compensate and more carefully consider your possible responses or actions.[16] With this in mind, managers should

Shannon D. Jones

complete the Implicit Association Test (IAT) developed at Harvard University. The IAT measures attitudes and beliefs that people may be unwilling or unable to report.[17] There are "ethical considerations individuals must consider when using test results, because the IAT may reveal troubling aspects of human nature."[18] The preferred use of IAT is for the individual to develop awareness of implicit preferences and stereotypes. For a better understanding of the IAT and unconscious bias in general, library leaders and their staff should read Mahzarin R. Binaji's *Blindspot: Hidden Biases of Good People.*[19] These strategies taken together are necessary for embarking on recruitment and retention activities for your library.

Recruitment

The war for talent is real in academic libraries. The competition is stiff, and the options are many. Statistics from the American Library Association (ALA) indicate that there are an estimated 119,487 libraries of all kinds in the United States, with 3,793 classified as academic libraries.[20] This means 3,793 academic libraries are vying for the very best individuals to join their teams. The most important library is the one in which you work. Any good manager wants to have the best of the best on his or her team. A guiding question to consider when thinking about recruiting personnel is: What would make someone want to work in your library? Answering this question requires a certain amount of thought and preparation.

Recruiting high-performing individuals to the library staff may require casting a wide net. Recruitment is a multipronged activity that requires a variety of strategies. The first and most important step in the recruitment process is to think about the skill set of the existing library staff. How does this measure against the current or emerging needs of your campus? The second step is assessing the existing vacancy to determine if the position is still needed, or if rewriting the job description is necessary. The third step is to create a recruitment plan. T. Y. Neely recommends libraries create a collaborative, cohesive, and holistic approach to harnessing available information and resources on recruitment, retention, and opportunities for advancement.[21] One key element of a recruitment strategy is a written recruitment plan that specifies the venues where the position will be posted. The rationale for creating a written plan is varied: it ensures that the marketing efforts are intentional and strategic; it requires the administrator to think about the places that will draw the most attention to the position; it provides a checklist for future reference; and, most importantly, it ensures that venues targeting underrepresented minorities are considered.

The plan should be customized for each position. A good recruitment strategy includes a combination of free and for-fee websites such as the ALA's JobLIST, the career centers of the Medical Library Association (MLA) and Special Library Association, and job boards for regional and state associations such as the Southern Chapter of the Medical Library Association and the South Carolina Library Association. Excellent venues for targeting underrepresented minorities include the African American Medical Librarians Alliance of the MLA, the American Indian Library Association, the Asian Pacific American Librarians Association, the Black Caucus of the American Library Association, the Chinese American Librarians Association, and the National Association for Promoting Library & Information Services to Latinos and the Spanish Speaking.

Promotion via library sciences electronic LISTSERVs is also a key element of a solid recruitment plan. For instance, when recruiting for a position targeting new and minority librarians, sending a message via the LISTSERVs of the ALA's Spectrum Scholars program or the Association of College and Research Libraries' (ACRL) Residency Interest Group are excellent places to start. The ALA's Spectrum Scholar program "recruits and provides scholarships to American Indian/Alaska Native, Asian, Black/African American, Hispanic/Latino and Native Hawaiian/Other Pacific Islander students to assist individuals interested in obtaining a graduate degree and leadership positions within the profession and our organization."[22] The ACRL Residency Interest Group is an assembly of library residents (both current and former), residency program coordinators, library deans, administrators, diversity officers, and human resources professionals from more than twenty different library systems across the country.[23]

Recruiting the best individual for a position is not a one-size-fits-all activity. For instance, when creating a written strategy, the advertising venues used for recruiting an instruction librarian are likely very different from those used when recruiting a systems librarian. Other strategies include soliciting nominations from colleagues, reviewing LinkedIn profiles, and sending the announcement to schools that have large enrollments of underrepresented minorities, including places like North Carolina Central University and the University of Arizona. Silent recruitment—a type of proactive networking—is another good strategy. While at conferences or serving on committees, it is common for librarians to meet other colleagues who would be an excellent addition to their own libraries—if they only had a position open. This is why it is helpful for administrators to have potential candidates in mind in the event a position does open up—when funding becomes available, for instance. This type of forward-thinking planning is essential for positioning the library as a strategic partner on campus.

Another aspect of recruiting quality employees is to carefully consider who serves on search committees. Universities have Equal Employment Opportunity standards and human resources procedures that must be followed when forming a search committee. With every search committee created, it is

　　　　　　　　　　　　　　　　Shannon D. Jones

important to assemble a group who can best assess applicants' suitability for employment within the library.

When forming a committee, one may want to consider the racial and ethnic makeup of librarianship as a whole. Statistics from the ALA's Diversity Counts Survey indicate that 85 percent of librarians are white females.[24] Diversity Counts is a comprehensive study of gender, race, and age in the library profession, originally conducted in 2006 and released in 2007. The study was updated in 2012 using 2009–2010 American Community Survey analyses. The new data reveals a small gain in the percentage of racial and ethnic minorities working as credentialed librarians—from 11 to 12 percent between 2000 and 2010. In 2009, there was a total of 118,666 credentialed librarians. Of this number there were 104,392 whites; 6,160 African Americans; 3,260 Asian and Pacific Islanders, Native Hawaiian, and other Pacific Islanders; 185 Native American, including Alaskan; 1,008 of two or more races; and 3,661 Latinos. In terms of gender, there were 98,273 females and 20,393 males, with 86,107 and 18,285 representing white females and males, respectively. A significant disparity exists in the number of males from traditionally underrepresented groups. The data shows the male demographic includes 563 African American; 787 Asian and Pacific Islanders, Native Hawaiian, and other Pacific Islanders; 8 Native American, including Alaskan; 181 of two or more races; and 522 Latinos.[25]

Given these statistics regarding diversity, it may be advantageous for administrators to form search committees that are as inclusive as possible. The goal is to ensure that individuals who serve on search committees represent a wide range of perspectives. Whenever possible, measures should be taken to ensure that every committee has at least one member from an underrepresented community on board. It is important that committee members have a keen understanding of what qualifications are required for the position. Library management should also explain to the search committee the importance of technical versus soft skills. A *technical skill* is "a skill that is required for the accomplishment of a specific task,"[26] while *soft skills* involve "communicating, conflict management, human relations, making presentations, negotiating, team building, and other such ability, defined in terms of expected outcomes and not as a specific method or technique such as statistical analysis."[27]

While the library can provide opportunities and tools to help an employee improve a technical skill such as searching, soft skills are harder to teach. The ever-changing environment of academia may offer little time to learn soft skills while on the job. In addition, while it is important that committee members prioritize core skills, they shouldn't discount other helpful skills the applicant may bring to the position. For example, an applicant with a strong marketing background can bring value to the library, especially if the library has historically struggled with promoting its services. Empowering a search committee to deviate from traditional or obvious skill sets is more important than ever. The current reality is that hiring a librarian with only a core or traditional skill set will no longer be sufficient. Today's medical libraries need to exhibit a strong commitment to find and to hire personnel with all the skills required to operate in the twenty-first century.

Retention

Anyone who has served on a search committee, has participated in candidate interviews, or has direct hiring responsibilities knows all too well the tremendous amount of time and energy it takes to complete the recruitment process. With this understanding, retaining high-performing staff is just as important as recruiting them to your organization. Creating an environment where library staff cannot only thrive, but also innovate, is a worthwhile goal for any library. Administrators must ensure that their personnel have the knowledge and tools needed to improve their performance and be as effective as possible. This cultivates an environment that will sustain or improve employees' job satisfaction and their desire to stay on with the organization.

In a 2015 LinkedIn post, Jennifer Anderson post stated that employees stay on when they are paid well, mentored, challenged, promoted, valued, mission orientated, empowered, and trusted. This highlights why it is important for organizations to take care of their employees and enable an environment that encourages discovery, learning, research, innovation, and growth. Simply put, happy employees are productive employees. It is important that administrators think about the conditions required to keep the library's personnel from seeking employment elsewhere. Senior administrators must spend some time thinking about the role they play in creating or supporting an environment where people thrive. A 2006 article from the *Harvard Business Review* reveals people leave their jobs because they don't like their boss, don't see opportunities for promotion or growth, or are offered a better gig (and often higher pay). These reasons have held steady for years.[28]

An earlier section of this chapter encouraged leaders to gain an awareness of how unconscious biases influences their decisions and actions. Knowing thyself means administrators should understand their leadership styles and preferences. A few strategies for doing so include completing tests such as Meyers-Briggs Type Indicator, or the Fundamental Interpersonal Relations Orientation. These tools help people understand their personalities, interpersonal needs, and communication styles. Another option is Gallup's StrengthsFinder Profile, which is a web-based interview that analyzes people's instinctive reactions and presents them with their five most dominant strengths. Regardless of which method is used, it is important that time is spent on self-discovery in order to recruit, retain, and develop staff effectively.

Staff retention starts the moment an individual joins the library team. It normally takes six to twelve months for a new employee to learn an organization's culture and his or her role within that organization. In the fast-paced health sciences environment, newly hired librarians do not always have the luxury of an extended orientation period and may be expected to assist patrons at a moment's notice, regardless of circumstance. This urgency is largely due to staffing shortages and competing priorities, which can be especially hard when the individual is still learning his or her job, the organization, and its people. Developing a formal orientation program, often known as onboarding, will assist in acclimating new personnel to the job.

The overall goal for an onboarding program is to shorten the acclimation period for new staff. A secondary goal for the program is to allow newly hired librarians to learn as much about the library's collections, services, and clientele as quickly as possible. Emphasis should be placed on the need for new personnel to gain an understanding of the library's mission and the schools and programs the library serves. The benefit of this orientation is that it will not only shorten the learning curve of new personnel, but will also ensure that vital processes and information are shared with new staff during their initial months on the job. Other retention strategies include: offering programs that address work culture issues; cultivating a positive environment; honoring employee values, opinions, and voices; providing opportunities for professional development; and recognizing work-life balance needs.[29] Ultimately, the goal of an orientation program is to remove some of the guesswork from learning about an organization, its people, its services, its collections, and its target audience.

Another retention strategy is to provide library personnel with opportunities to grow their skill sets by way of professional development and continuing education. One method to accomplish this is to encourage new faculty librarians to create a two-to-three-year personal development plan that identifies long- and short-term goals. This process has a number of benefits: it requires the librarian to think about his or her future goals; it helps the supervisor to advise and support the librarian in reaching the identified goals; it helps the supervisor assure that the goals align with the library's strategy; it allows the supervisor to make recommendations about professional development opportunities; and it gives the librarian a roadmap to check his or her progress. For example, a librarian who has a goal of participating in systematic reviews might be encouraged to complete the University of Pittsburgh Systematic Review Workshop as the foundation for this goal.

A key element of any discussion regarding retention is promotion and tenure. Whether an institution is a publish-or-perish or a publish-and-flourish environment, there are core strategies that an administrator can recommend to help the librarian prepare for this important career goal. The most important and beneficial strategy is to have the librarian begin preparing from day one. B. Kim offers ten practical tips librarians may find helpful when compiling their promotion or tenure files, including obtaining a copy of the library's promotion/tenure policy, having an awareness of the criteria and eligibility to apply for promotion or tenure, soliciting advice assistance from librarians who have gone through the process, collecting and gathering documentation under the same categories that the application file requires, keeping documentation, updating CVs and lists of continuing education activities regularly, collecting letters for committee appointment and other service activities, reviewing dates in the application timeline, and planning ahead.[30] Organization is key.

The literature is replete with articles that discuss the benefits of mentorship on professional growth. There are many benefits of formal and informal mentorship relationships. Effective mentoring is essential to the growth and success of librarianship in all types of library.[31] B. Farrell et al. note that libraries have often utilized informal and formal mentorship programs to acclimate new employees and encourage the sharing of professional knowledge between more experienced librarians and their newer colleagues.[32] S. Freedman adds that research libraries, which foster a culture of learning, increasingly look at mentoring as a professional development effort as well as a way to retain workers and deal with the massive retirement of librarians.[33] According to Freedman, the benefits of mentoring for librarians include increased employee retention, reduced turnover, faster induction, guidance in organizational expectations, and improved leadership.[34] Mentoring can help library organizations recruit, retain, and revitalize the library workforce, as well as engage them in a continuous learning process for professional development.[35]

Benefits for mentees include the opportunity to interact and learn from mentors within a nonthreatening relationship. Outcomes of this support, which builds confidence and maintains motivation, include developing skills and knowledge, solving problems, determining how and where to find further information, exploring career options, and learning coping strategies.[36]

A. V. Level writes that participation in professional organizations offers important opportunities to network, learn, and share knowledge.[37] Professional organizations are an excellent venue to identify potential mentors. Many professional organizations offer some type of mentorship program. For instance, the MLA offers a mentor database that librarians at all levels may use to identify mentors or seek guidance on a variety of topics, including membership in the Academy of Health Information Professionals, changing specialties within the profession, or becoming a medical librarian. The MLA also offers a Colleague Connection Program that pairs mentees with more experienced mentors in a conference setting.

Reward and Recognition

Many library administrators know all too well that providing meaningful rewards for staff who go above and beyond presents a significant challenge in a time of shrinking budgets. B. Nelson posits that at a time when employees are asked to do more than ever before—to make suggestions for continuous improvement, resolve complex problems quickly, and act independently in the best interest of the company—most companies have fewer resources to commit to such practices, given the challenging economic environment in recent years.[38] It is unlikely that all libraries are able to give monetary incentives to exemplary personnel, so creating a rewarding work environment that fosters positive experiences is paramount. In many cases, this kind of environment is equally important as—if not more important than—monetary rewards. It takes work to identify what motivates members of the library staff to do a good job. Because these factors will be different for every member of your staff, a variety of strategies will need to be employed. Nelson noted that it does not take a fat bonus check, a trip to the Bahamas, or a lavish annual awards banquet to get the best out of people; it just takes a little time, thoughtfulness, and energy to make a difference in an employee's job. Rewards and recognition are tools that can be used by any manager to realize important benefits.[39] There are a number of strategies that may be helpful in rewarding library personnel for a job well done.

Expressions of Gratitude

It is amazing how far a simple thank-you goes in bolstering an employee's confidence in the workplace. While most of us are busy, it is immensely important that managers and leaders alike take the time to express their gratitude and appreciation when staff members go above and beyond the call of duty. Thank-you cards, e-mail applause, and public recognition in meetings are visible demonstrations of appreciation and gratitude. R. A. Sansone writes that experiencing gratitude, thankfulness, and appreciation tends to foster positive feelings, which in turn contribute to one's overall sense of well-being.[40]

Professional Development

As a library administrator, it is important to provide the tools and resources that staff need in order to do their best work. To acknowledge and recognize staff's desire for self-improvement, the MUSC Library has committed a portion of the budget toward continuing professional development. Development opportunities can range from providing funding for conference attendance; arranging webinars from the ALA, ACRL, or MLA; bringing speakers to the library; or allocating release time to attend on- and off-campus workshops. The likely return on investment for the library is new excitement from the staff regarding their work. A. V. Level notes that making sure that new librarians have several venues to pursue for professional development and continuing education will contribute to improved job performance and retention.[41] Administrators are encouraged to "offer these opportunities so that librarians at all levels feel they are effective in their positions."[42]

Paraprofessionals, whose work experience may be limited, should be encouraged to attend outside conferences or workshops in order to gain a fresh perspective about their work and contributions, and to better understand the logic behind the need for change. In addition to networking opportunities, conference exposure reveals alternative work methods and strategies that attendees can compare to their own experiences. It is more difficult to see a vision for the future without looking outside your own library. Unfortunately, paraprofessionals are often excluded from these activities, as many libraries limit participation to their professional personnel, but exposure to the outer world can be a plus for all staff members as libraries continue to transition in the new millennium.

Staff Engagement

One of the greatest joys an administrator can have is connecting with staff members on a personal level. It is important for administrators to know their staff and learn more about the work they do for the library. One strategy that may be helpful is to occasionally shadow staff throughout the library. This was recently done at the MUSC Library with its interlibrary loan and document delivery staff. These interactions provide an opportunity to express gratitude for work done, ask questions about their work, and get feedback regarding how the administration can provide better support. As a result of this activity in the MUSC Library, administrators were made aware of the need for a dual-monitor setup. A week later, e-mails from several of the staff expressed appreciation for the new equipment—an investment that made their job easier and thus increased productivity.

Work-Life Balance

Encouraging a positive work-life balance is a helpful reward for staff. Being flexible with work schedules and allowing staff to take time off as needed goes a long way to ensure a positive work environment.

Shannon D. Jones

Voice at the Table

Providing opportunities for staff participation in decision making can be beneficial for any library. When the MUSC Library was developing its strategic plan, for example, information-gathering sessions were held with staff. A consultant led an exercise focused on the AI model. Feedback from staff revealed that they felt more connected to the plan because they had helped create it. In addition, staff came away with a clearer picture of how their work related to the library's overall goals.

University Recognition Opportunities

Many universities have mechanisms in place that allow managers and other employees to acknowledge the hard work their colleagues have done. For instance, the MUSC Applause Program recognizes employees who go the extra mile in providing quality service, education, research, and patient care. Anyone can complete a form to give an "applause" for a job well done. Several MUSC Library staff members have received this recognition from coworkers and library patrons over the years. In a time when budgets are tight and employees are expected to do more, it is important for managers to recognize personnel for doing a good job. Recognition can come in many forms, but more than ever, employees need to be told their efforts are appreciated and that they play an important role in their organizations.

Conclusion

The war to hire the best talent in libraries is real. Maintaining a competitive university requires medical libraries to actively recruit and retain great employees. This necessitates taking thoughtful and deliberate steps to ensure the library has the right talent at each level of staffing. This chapter has presented a number of practical strategies administrators and hiring managers can consider in recruiting, retaining, and rewarding high-performing employees—the best offense in the battle to maintain the highest level of service.

Notes

1. "Gap," Merriam-Webster.com, accessed December19 2016, https://www.merri am-webster.com/dictionary/gap.
2. D. L. Cooperrider and D. K. Whitney, *Appreciative Inquiry: A Positive Revolution in Change* (San Francisco: Berrett-Koehler, 2005), 8.
3. Ibid., 12.
4. Ibid., 15.
5. J. Peterson, "What Are the Most Common Hiring Mistakes?" *Insights from Stanford Business*, July 16, 2013, accessed March 19, 2017, https://www.gsb.stanford.edu/ insights/joel-peterson-what-are-most-common-hiring-mistakes.

6. Ibid.
7. J. Moule, "Understanding Unconscious Bias and Inintentional Racism," *Phi Delta Kappa* 90, no. 5 (2009): 321.
8. Eric Kofi Acree et al., (2001) "Using Professional Development as a Retention Tool for Underrepresented Academic Librarians," *Journal of Library Administration* 33, no. 1-2 (2001): 49.
9. "Unconscious Bias," University of California, San Francisco, Office of Diversity and Outreach, accessed March 19, 2017, https://diversity.ucsf.edu/resources/uncon scious-bias.
10. Moule, "Understanding Unconscious Bias and Unintentional Racism," 321.
11. Ibid., 323.
12. B. W. Collins, "Tackling Unconscious Bias in Hiring Practices: The Plight of the Rooney Rule," *New York University Law Review* 82 (2007): 870.
13. Ibid., 872.
14. Ibid., 908.
15. Mahzarin R. Banaji, Max H. Bazerman, and Dolly Chugh. "How (Un)ethical Are You?" *Harvard Business Review* 81, no. 12 (December 2003), 56.
16. Moule, "Understanding Unconscious Bias and Unintentional Racism," 320-26.
17. Project Implicit website, accessed March 19, 2017, https://implicit.harvard.edu/implicit/education.html.
18. Ibid.
19. M. R. Banaji and A. G. Greenwald, *Blindspot: Hidden Biases of Good People* (New York: Delacorte Press, 2013).
20. American Library Association, "Number of Libraries in the United States," ALA Library Fact Sheet 1, September 2015, accessed March 19, 2017, http://www.ala.org/tools/libfactsheets/alalibraryfactsheet01.
21. T. Y. Neely and L. Peterson, "Achieving Racial and Ethnic Diversity among Academic and Research Librarians: The Recruitment, Retention, and Advancement of Librarians of Color—A White Paper," *College & Research Libraries News* 68, no. 9 (2007): 563.
22. ALA Spectrum Scholarship Program website, accessed March 20, 2017, http://www.ala.org/offices/diversity/spectrum.
23. "About Us," ACRL Residency Interest Group website, accessed March 20, 2017, http://acrl.ala.org/residency/?page_id=418.
24. American Library Association, "Diversity Counts 2012 Tables," accessed October 13, 2014.
25. Ibid.
26. "Technical Skill," BusinessDictionary.com, accessed January 1, 2017, http://www.businessdictionary.com/definition/technical-skills.html.
27. "Soft Skill," BusinessDictionary.com, accessed January 2, 2017, http://www.businessdictionary.com/definition/soft-skill.html.
28. "Why People Quit Their Jobs," *Harvard Business Review*, September 2016, accessed March 19, 2017, https://hbr.org/2016/09/why-people-quit-their-jobs.
29. Neely and Peterson, "Achieving Racial and Ethnic Diversity among Academic and Research Librarians," 564.
30. B. Kim, "10 Practical Tips for Compiling Your Promotion or Tenure File," ACRL Tech-Connect (blog), September 23, 2013, accessed March 28, 2017, http://acrl.ala.org/techconnect/post/practical-tips-on-assembling-your-promotion-or-tenure-file.

31. S. Freedman, "Effective Mentoring," *IFLA Journal* 35, no. 2 (2009): 172.
32. B. Farrell et al., "Addressing Psychosocial Factors with Library Mentoring," *Portal: Libraries and the Academy*, 17, no. 1 (2017): 51-69.
33. Freedman, "Effective Mentoring," 172.
34. Ibid., 173.
35. Ibid., 172.
36. Ibid., 173.
37. A. V. Level and J. Blair, "Holding On to Our Own: Factors Affecting the Recruitment and Retention of Science Librarians," *Science & Technology Libraries*, 27, no. 1-2 (2007): 194.
38. B. Nelson, (2016). "You Get What You Reward: A Research-Based Approach to Employee Recognition," in *The Psychologically Healthy Workplace: Building a Win-Win Environment for Organizations and Employees*, ed. M. Grawitch and D. Ballard (Washington, DC: American Psychological Association, 2016), 158.
39. Ibid., 159.
40. R. A. Sansone and L. A. Sansone, "Gratitude and Well-Being: The Benefits of Appreciation," *Psychiatry (1550-5952)*, 7, no. 11 (2010): 19.
41. Level and Blair, "Holding On to Our Own," 194.
42. Ibid.

Further Reading

"About Us." ACRL Residency Interest Group website. Accessed March 20, 2017. http://acrl.ala.org/residency/?page_id=418.

Acree, E. K., S. K. Epps, Y. Gilmore, and C. Henriques. "Using Professional Development as a Retention Tool for Underrepresented Academic Librarians." *Journal of Library Administration* 33, no. 1-2 (2001): 45-61.

ALA Spectrum Scholarship Program website. Accessed March 20, 2017. http://www.ala.org/offices/diversity/spectrum.

American Library Association. "Diversity Counts 2009-2010 Update." ALA Office for Diversity website. Accessed November 21, 2012. http://www.Ala.org/offices/diversity/diversitycounts/2009-2010update.

———. "Number of Libraries in the United States." ALA Library Fact Sheet 1. September 2015. Accessed March 21, 2017, http://www.ala.org/tools/libfact-sheets/alalibraryfactsheet01.

Banaji, Mahzarin R., Max H. Bazerman, and Dolly Chugh." How (Un)ethical Are You?" *Harvard Business Review* 81, no. 12 (December 2003), 56-64.

Banaji, M. R., and A. G. Greenwald. *Blindspot: Hidden Biases of Good People*. New York: Delacorte Press, 2013.

Bugg, K. (2016). "The Perceptions of People of Color in Academic Libraries concerning the Relationship between Retention and Advancement as Middle Managers." *Journal of Library Administration* 56, no. 4 (2016): 428–43.

Collins, B. W. "Tackling Unconscious Bias in Hiring Practices: The Plight of the Rooney Rule." *New York University Law Review* 82 (2007): 870.

Cooperrider, D. L., and D. K. Whitney. *Appreciative Inquiry: A Positive Revolution in Change.* San Francisco: Berrett-Koehler, 2005.

Farrell, B., J. Alabi, P. Whaley, and C. Jenda. "Addressing Psychosocial Factors with Library Mentoring."*Portal: Libraries and the Academy* 17, no. 1 (2017): 51–69.

Freedman, S. "Effective Mentoring." *IFLA Journal* 35, no. 2 (2009): 171–82.

Kim, B. "10 Practical Tips for Compiling Your Promotion or Tenure File." ACRL TechConnect (blog), September 23, 2013. Accessed March 28, 2017, http:// acrl.ala.org/techconnect/post/practical-tips-on-assembling-your-promotion-or-tenure-file.

Level, A. V., and J. Blair. "Holding On to Our Own: Factors Affecting the Recruitment and Retention of Science Librarians." *Science & Technology Libraries* 27, no. 1–2 (2007): 185–202.

Moule, J. "Understanding Unconscious Bias and Unintentional Racism." *Phi Delta Kappa* 90, no. 5 (2009): 320–26.

Neely, T. Y., and L. Peterson. "Achieving Racial and Ethnic Diversity among Academic and Research Librarians: The Recruitment, Retention, and Advancement of Librarians of Color—A White Paper."*College & Research Libraries News* 68, no. 9 (2007): 562–65.

Nelson, B. "You Get What You Reward: A Research-Based Approach to Employee Recognition." In *The Psychologically Healthy Workplace: Building a Win-Win Environment for Organizations and Employees,* edited by M. Grawitch and D. Ballard, 157–79. Washington, DC: American Psychological Association, 2016.

Peterson, J. "What Are the Most Common Hiring Mistakes?" *Insights from Stanford Business.* July 16, 2013. Accessed March 19, 2017, https://www.gsb.stan ford.edu/insights/joel-peterson-what-are-most-common-hiring-mistakes.

Shannon D. Jones

Project Implicit website. Accessed March 19, 2017. https://implicit.harvard.edu/implicit/education.html.

Ross, K. M. (2013). "Purposeful Mentoring in Academic Libraries."*Journal of Library Administration* 53, no. 7-8 (2013): 412-28.

Sansone R. A. and L. A. Sansone. "Gratitude and Well-Being: The Benefits of Appreciation."*Psychiatry* 7, no. 11 (2010): 18-22.

Snyder, L., and E. Crane. (2016). "Developing and Implementing an Onboarding Program for an Academic Library: Strategies and Methods." *Library Leadership & Management* 30, no. 3 (2016): 1-3.

"Unconscious Bias." University of California, San Francisco, Office of Diversity and Outreach. Accessed March 19, 2017. https://diversity.ucsf.edu/resources/unconscious-bias.

Weiner, S. "Setting the Stage for Success: Developing an Orientation Program for Academic Library Faculty." *Library Leadership & Management* 30, no. 1 (2015): 1-24.

"Why People Quit Their Jobs." *Harvard Business Review*, August 23, 2016. Accessed March 19, 2017. https://hbr.org/2016/09/why-people-quit-their-jobs.

Index

staff hiring and recruitment, xviii, 11, 48, 74, 76, 95, 115, 117–20
staff morale, 106
staff motivation, xvi–xviii, 73, 80–82, 109
staff participation, 98, 126
staff potential, 115
staff preparation, xi
staff readiness, 90
staff reductions, xvi
staff restructuring, xvii
staff retention, xviii, 95, 115, 117–18, 122
staff satisfaction, xviii
staff self discovery, xviii
staff self-improvement, xvi
staff skills, 104, 115, 119
staff strengths and weaknesses, xvii, 73
staff stress, 105–6
staff training, xvi, 10, 30, 31, 34–35, 48–49, 62–63
staffing gaps, 115–116
Stanford Graduate School of Business, 117
Steers, R. M., 23
Steffens, N. K., 105
stereotypes, 117
Stony Brook University libraries, 91–92
strategic planning, 45, 93–94, 106, 116, 127
StrengthsFinder Profile (Gallup), 84–85, 122
stress, 106
subject specialist librarian model, 95
support staff, 37–39, 65–70
Support Staff Interests Round Table, American library Association, 38
survey, 104
Swim Lane, 49
systems approach, 90–91

"tea time training", 35
teaching and learning outcomes, 98
teamwork, xvi, 77, 82
technical services, xv
technical skills, 78–79, 121
text mining, 99

therapeutics, xi
Thomas, K. W., 16, 18, 20, 82
3-D modeling and printing, 47, 89–90, 99
time management, 104–105, 111
training assessment, 35
training, online, xvi, 36, 38–39
transparency, 24
triage library support, 98
trust, xvi, 22–23 49–50, 70–71

unconscious bias, 117, 118
unions, xvii, 12, 65–71
University of Arizona, 89, 100, 120
University of Iowa, 37
upskilling, 104
user expectations, management of, 1, 104

verbal communication, 59
Velthouse, B. A., 16, 18, 20
virtual reality, 90
vision, 116–17

Webb, Margaret, 29
WebEx, 61
WebJunction, 31
wellness, 106
Werner, Susan E., 91
Wilkinson, Mike, 34
Williams, Karen, 94, 95, 96
work as play, 81
work ethic, 80
work styles, xvii, 73
workflow, xv, 91, 103–5, 107, 111
work-life balance, 105, 126
workplace design, 46
workshops, xvi, 36
writing service, 75

Yale University, xv
Yale University library system, xv
Yale-New Haven Hospital, 5
Yammer, 61
Yerkes, Leslie, 82
Yukl, G.A., 16, 18, 22, 25

About the Editors and Contributors

Melanie J. Norton, MLIS, is head of access and delivery services at the Harvey Cushing/John Hay Whitney Medical Library at Yale University. A librarian for more than thirty-five years, she began her professional career as a reference librarian at Rochester Institute of Technology and a liaison to the faculty and students at the National Institute for the Deaf, one of the nine schools supported by the library. She learned sign language, wrote numerous articles, and edited a special edition of *Library Trends* (summer 1992): *Libraries Serving an Underserved Population: Deaf and Hearing Impaired Patrons.* The University of North Carolina at Chapel Hill offered her an opportunity to work in their Health Sciences Library as head of the Interlibrary Loan Department. During her thirteen years there, she served as president of the Association of North Carolina Health Sciences Librarians and chair of the Mid-Atlantic Chapter of the Medical Library Association. In 2011, Melanie accepted a position as head of interlibrary loan at the Cushing/Whitney Medical Library at Yale University. She moved into the position of head of access and delivery services that same year. She continues to be involved professionally by serving on MLA committees and the Executive Committee of the North Atlantic Chapter of the MLA.

Nathan Rupp, MLIS, MBA, is the head of collection development and management at the Harvey Cushing/John Hay Whitney Medical Library at Yale University, where he has worked since 2012. He is responsible for coordinating collection development, acquisitions, and cataloging for the medical library, and also supports scholarly communications efforts for the library. He has a wide range of experience in collection development and technical services at several ARL libraries and has held leadership positions in the American Library Association, Special Libraries Association, and the North Atlantic Health Sciences Libraries association. He has written articles on technical services, digital libraries, and collection development.

★ ★ ★

Michael Brewer, MA, MLIS, is head of research and learning at the University of Arizona Libraries. Before moving into administrative roles beginning in 2008, he served as a subject librarian for Slavic studies, as well as for German studies and media arts. He has been engaged as a scholar on a wide range of topics, including information literacy, copyright, competencies, and assessment, among others. He is past chair of the Committee on Library and Information Resources for the Association for Slavic, East European, and Eurasian Studies and of the Copyright Education Committee of the ALA's Office for Information Technology Policy.

Amy Blevins, MALS, currently works at the Ruth Lilly Medical Library as the associate director for public services. Amy is a longtime member of the Medical Library Association, currently serves as a member of the MLA Board of Directors as well as the incoming treasurer for the association. She has served in numerous leadership positions for the Educational Media and Technologies section for MLA and is the past-chair of the Professional Recruitment and Retention Committee. She has more than a decade of experience with teaching longitudinal curriculum-based sessions in academic health sciences libraries. She has taught continuing education sessions on instructional design, is one of the coeditors of the book *Curriculum-Based Library Instruction,* and has published several articles on online tutorials and distance education.

Ryan Harris, MLIS, AHIP serves as the reference service manager, research and education librarian at the University of Maryland, Baltimore. In this role, he supervises information services staff and a variety of services, including the library's IRB Consent Form Review Service, workshops, and poster printing. He is also actively involved in teaching and systematic review services. He is an active member of the Medical Library Association. He has served as chair of the Relevant Issues Section and the Membership Committee. He has also served as chair of the Mid-Atlantic Chapter of the Medical Library Association.

Heather N. Holmes, MLIS, AHIP, is the associate director of libraries at the Medical University of South Carolina. She received her master of library and information science degree from the University of Pittsburgh in 1998. She is a 2010 recipient of the National Library of Medicine's biomedical informatics fellowship held in Woods Hole, Massachusetts, and was named one of *Library Journal*'s Movers & Shakers for 2011. She is a Distinguished Member of the Academy of Health Information Professionals and the 2014 recipient of the Lois Ann Colaianni Award for Excellence and Achievement in Hospital Librarianship. She is passionate about clinical librarianship and continues to mentor others who are just breaking into the specialization.

Dixie A. Jones, MLS, AHIP, recently retired as director of the Health Sciences Library at LSU Health Shreveport. Her experience has included libraries in a nursing school, a hospital, and a school of medicine. For forty-two years, health sciences librarianship has been her passion, culminating with the presidency of the Medical Library Association in 2014. Participating in this book was a pleasure, as she believes that the staff is the most important component of any medical library. She is looking forward to seeing transformations in librarians' roles in the future.

Shannon D. Jones, MLS, MEd, AHIP, is the director of libraries for the Medical University of South Carolina Libraries in Charleston. She earned her MLS from North Carolina Central University. Shannon also holds a MEd in adult learning from Virginia Commonwealth University. Shannon's research interests include staff recruitment and retention, organizational learning and development, and leadership in academic health sciences libraries.

Elizabeth Kiscaden, MLIS, is the associate director of the National Network of Libraries of Medicine, Greater Midwest Region Office, and has been a health sciences librarian for nearly a decade. Originally from Minnesota, she worked at the Mayo Clinic in the Center for Translational Science Activities before relocating to Iowa. She started her career in librarianship as a solo hospital librarian at Mercy Medical Center–North Iowa in Mason City. Following this, she served as an academic library director at a small liberal arts college before returning to health sciences librarianship as the head of library services at Hardin Library for the Health Sciences. Since 2016, she has served as the associate director of the NNLM office for the upper Midwest, an office funded through the University of Iowa and located in Hardin Library.

Teresa L. Knott, MLS, MPA, AHIP, is the director of the Tompkins-McCaw Library for the Health Sciences at Virginia Commonwealth University and associate university librarian for the VCU Libraries. She holds master's degrees in library science from the University of Oklahoma and public administration from the University of Texas at El Paso. Before joining VCU, she held administrative positions at Texas Tech University Health Sciences Center at El Paso's

Library of the Health Sciences and at the University of Maryland, Baltimore's Health Sciences and Human Services Library. She has long-standing interests in leadership development, personnel management, and emerging technologies.

Elaine R. Martin, MSLS, DA, is the director and chief administrative officer at Harvard Medical School's Francis A. Countway Library of Medicine. Prior to Harvard, she served eighteen years as the director of library services for the Lamar Soutter Library at the University of Massachusetts Medical School in Worcester, where she led the library through a period of transformational change and is currently in the process of developing a new strategic plan for Harvard's Countway Library. She has also served as the director of library services of the National Network of Libraries of Medicine, New England Region, from 2001 to 2016.

Meaghan Muir, MLIS, is the manager of library services at Boston Children's Hospital. She has more than fifteen years of experience working in medical libraries. Previous affiliations include Spaulding Rehabilitation Hospital and Brigham and Women's Hospital, both in Boston. She is professionally active in the North Atlantic Health Sciences Libraries, Regional Chapter of the Medical Library Association. She holds a master's degree in library and information science from the University of Rhode Island. She is professionally active in the North Atlantic Health Sciences Libraries, Regional Chapter of the Medical Library Association.

Gerald Perry, MLS, AHIP, is associate dean for health sciences and strategic planning for the University of Arizona Libraries. As associate dean for health sciences, he is the director of the University of Arizona Health Sciences Library. In his role as associate dean for strategic planning, he is responsible for coordinating strategic planning and related assessment efforts across the UAL system. He is also responsible for coordinating diversity and inclusion efforts at UAL. All the research and learning librarians across the UAL system report to him through their departmental head or supervisor. He has more than thirty years of experience as a health sciences librarian and has been active in the Medical Library Association, having served as president (2011–2012). Academic interests include leadership and administration, informatics, evidence-based practice, and diversity and inclusion.

Ana Reeves, MLIS, is a research and education services informationist for the Medical University of South Carolina Libraries in Charleston. She holds the master of library and information science degree from San José State University in California and the bachelor of arts in learning, culture, and self-expression from Western Washington University in Bellingham. Her work with MUSC involves communications and marketing in the library and across campus, implementation

About the Editors and Contributors

and management of LibGuides, and teaching library resources to staff and the campus as a whole.

Jean P. Shipman, MSLS, AHIP, FMLA, is the vice president, global library relations, for Elsevier. Prior to that she was the executive director, knowledge management and Spencer S. Eccles Health Sciences Library; director of the Mid-Continental Region and National Training Office of the National Network of Libraries of Medicine; director for information transfer, Center of Medical Innovation; and adjunct faculty of the Department of Biomedical Informatics, School of Medicine, all at the University of Utah. She has also been employed by the John Hopkins University, Greater Baltimore Medical Center, University of Maryland, University of Washington, and Virginia Commonwealth University. She served as president of the Medical Library Association for 2006–2007 and on the board of directors for the Society for Scholarly Publishing from 2013 until 2016. She was a member and co-chair of the Chicago Collaborative, a group of publishers, librarians, and editors who met to discuss issues regarding scholarly communications. She is the coeditor of two books: *Information and Innovation: A Natural Combination for Health Sciences Libraries* and *Strategic Collaborations in Health Sciences Libraries.*

Meredith Solomon, MLS, AHIP, is associate librarian at Brigham and Women's Hospital in Boston. She has more than twenty years of experience working in academic, public, and medical libraries. Previous affiliations include the National Network of Libraries of Medicine, New England Region; University of Massachusetts Medical School; INOVA Healthcare; University of Maryland, Baltimore; and National Library of Medicine, associate fellow. She holds a master's degree in library and information management from Emporia University in Kansas and is a senior member of the Academy of Health Information Professionals.

Mary Joan (M. J.) Tooey, MLS, AHIP, FMLA, is associate vice president, Academic Affairs, and executive director of the Health Sciences and Human Services Library at the University of Maryland, Baltimore. She is the director of the National Network of Libraries of Medicine's Southeastern Atlantic Region and the National DOCLINE Coordination Office. She served as president of the Medical Library Association (2005–2006) and the Association of Academic Health Sciences Libraries (2012–2013). She is a Fellow of MLA and a Distinguished Member of the Academy of Health Information Professionals. She received the 1997 MLA Estelle Brodman Award and was the 2016 MLA Janet Doe Lecturer. In 2011, she received the Distinguished Alumni Award from the University of Pittsburgh's iSchool.

CPSIA information can be obtained
at www.ICGtesting.com
Printed in the USA
BVHW01*2332081217
502140BV00001B/1/P

9 781442 272194